"Jonathan Wilson's insightful and i
calls Christians to faithful discip.
significant interest in the virtues fi
thought, and he rightly transforms tl
important ways. I recommend _. _......ustasucally."

L. GREGORY JONES
Dean of the Divinity School
Duke University

"This book is exceptional in its clarity and helpfulness.
Jonathan Wilson provides a compelling account of the
distinctive characteristics and practices connected with
the gospel-shaped virtues of faith, hope and love.
Against the backdrop of a nuanced presentation of
contemporary culture in its modern and postmodern expression,
Wilson offers a refreshingly thoughtful description of
a thoroughly Christian way of life."

CHRISTINE D. POHL
Professor of Social Ethics
Asbury Theological Seminary

"Efforts to promote an ethics of 'virtue' or 'character' have
sometimes been hampered by inadequate accounts of Christian
particularity or by inaccessibility to nonspecialists.
Jonathan Wilson addresses both deficits, and more:
he responds to valid evangelical concerns about the dangers of
virtue language, and he shows how Christian virtues should
shape (and be shaped by) concrete practices. I hope that
Gospel Virtues will be read, across denominational lines,
by pastors, seminarians, lay leaders and—dare I say it?—
by those ethicists who haven't yet heard the 'good news'!"

DAVID S. CUNNINGHAM
Associate Professor of Theology and Ethics
Seabury-Western Theological Seminary

"Most books about virtue ethics are meant for scholars
to debate. Jonathan Wilson's *Gospel Virtues* is meant for churches
to use. With intellectual rigor and theological precision, he shows
what is distinctive about the Christian virtues of faith and hope
and love, and how they are to be practiced in the churches
through education and worship and hospitality."

RALPH WOOD
Professor of Religion and Literature
Baylor University

GOSPEL VIRTUES

Practicing Faith,
Hope & Love
in Uncertain Times

JONATHAN R. WILSON

InterVarsity Press
Downers Grove, Illinois

InterVarsity Press
P.O. Box 1400, Downers Grove, IL 60515
World Wide Web: www.ivpress.com
E-mail: mail@ivpress.com

InterVarsity Press® is the book-publishing division of InterVarsity Christian Fellowship®, a
student movement active on campus at hundreds of universities, colleges and schools of nursing
in the United States of America, and a member movement of the International Fellowship of
Evangelical Students. For information about local and regional activities, write Public
Relations Dept., InterVarsity Christian Fellowship, 6400 Schroeder Rd., P.O. Box 7895, Madison,
WI 53707-7895.

Scripture quotations, unless otherwise noted, are from the New Revised Standard Version of the
Bible, copyright 1989 by the Division of Christian Education of the National Council of the
Churches of Christ in the U.S.A., and are used by permission.

Excerpt from "Manifesto: The Mad Farmer Liberation Front" from THE COUNTRY OF
MARRIAGE, copyright © 1973 by Wendell Berry, reprinted by permission of Harcourt Brace &
Company.

Cover photograph: SuperStock

ISBN 0-8308-1520-1

Printed in the United States of America ♾

Library of Congress Cataloging-in-Publication Data

Wilson, Jonathan R.
    Gospel virtues : practicing faith, hope, and love in uncertain
times / Jonathan R. Wilson.
        p.   cm.
    Includes bibliographical references and index.
    ISBN 0-8308-1520-1 (pbk. : alk. paper)
    1. Theological virtues.   2. Christianity and culture.   I. Title.
BV4635.W55   1998
241'.4—dc21   98-11312
                                                                                    CIP

19   18   17   16   15   14   13   12   11   10   9   8   7   6   5   4   3   2   1

14   13   12   11   10   09   08   07   06   05   04   03   02   01   00   99   98

For
Leah

Acknowledgments

If this book is an expression of my life and calling, then I am indebted to more people than I can possibly acknowledge. At several points I write about the centrality of community in the formation of virtue. So I am indebted to the many communities that have been willing to share in my life: the congregations that my father pastored as I was growing up; the missionaries and staff of the Free Will Baptist Foreign Mission Department, 1961-1975; the people (and pastors, though they too are people) of Donelson Free Will Baptist Church (Nashville), First Baptist Church (Vancouver, B.C.), Edmonds Baptist Church (Burnaby, B.C.), Durham (N.C.) Mennonite Church and Montecito Covenant Church (Santa Barbara); and the faculty, staff and students of Free Will Baptist Bible College (1969-1975), Regent College (1975-1985), Duke University (1986-1989) and Westmont College (1989-1997).

The ideas in this book have been presented in various forms to several congregations: First Presbyterian Church, Santa Barbara; Montecito Covenant Church; First Baptist Church, Oxnard; Bethany Congregational Church, Santa Barbara; and Santa Barbara Community Church. I am indebted to these congregations for their comments and enthusiasm for the work. They have been a source of strength. I am particularly indebted to the generosity of Santa Barbara Community Church for the freedom I had to work on this book instead of supplementing my salary by teaching summer school.

I have also been taught by a close community of friends, many of whom have read all or portions of this book and contributed to it through their criticism and encouragement: Marti Wilson,

Greg Jones, Stanley Hauerwas, Bob Gundry, Shirley Mullen, Reggie and Stacy Williams, Lois Gundry and Serena Gideon.

My wife, Marti, encourages my writing and celebrates my eccentricities. The writing muse strikes me regularly between 10 p.m. and 2 a.m.—not a good schedule for a professional woman who likes her husband beside her when she sleeps. Marti is truly a woman of virtue, and I have often had her life in mind as I wrote these pages.

This book is dedicated to our daughter, Leah. We are grateful for the communities of faith, hope and love that have nurtured her. We pray that she and her generation will, by God's grace, be more faithful witnesses to the gospel than we have been.

Introduction   *does this adequately describe mission?*

The mission of the church of Jesus Christ is to bear witness, everywhere and always, to the gospel—the good news of salvation in Jesus Christ. That mission is carried out by the church through the power of the Holy Spirit. Although the mission and the source of the power never change, the context within which the church pursues her mission does change. New contexts bring new challenges and new opportunities for witnessing to the gospel. As Western culture goes through tumultuous changes, the church, in order to be a faithful witness of the gospel, must analyze those changes if she is to discern both threats to and opportunities for living out the gospel.

In this book I make use of the insights of virtue ethics to offer guidance for faithful witness in the midst of the changes taking place in our world. Although I will make considerable use of the tradition of virtue ethics, my purpose is not to offer a comprehensive treatment of that tradition. Rather, my purpose is to use virtue ethics to identify several ways through which we may recover faithful witness to the gospel in the life of the church. My allegiance is to the gospel and to the witness of the church, not to virtue ethics and the creation of a more moral society. What we need are not better lives but more faithful lives, not a more moral society but a more faithful church.

To be more faithful, the church's life must be grounded in a profound understanding of the gospel that comes through our participation in God's work of redemption. Since our participation in God's redemption occurs in the midst of a particular time and place, we must attend to our cultural situation if we are to be faithful. Such attention is not a surrender to the culture but a recognition of its dangers and opportunities.

When we do not attend to our cultural situation, our life and witness are liable to all kinds of unrecognized corruptions. When we do attend to the culture, we are better able to live and witness faithfully. Witnessing faithfully does not mean trimming the gospel so that it fits the demands of our culture. It does mean living out the good news of Jesus Christ in ways that the culture understands, even if it does not like or accept our message.

So this book is in part an ethic of virtue and in part a critique of culture. But its primary aim is to enable the church to witness faithfully to the gospel through the way that we live. It is not a handbook of Christian virtue ethics, for I do not attempt to cover systematically every issue raised by virtue ethics. It is also not a handbook of cultural analysis, for I leave many cultural issues and questions untouched.

Gospel Virtues is primarily a guide to faithful Christian living and witness. I draw on the three theological virtues of the Christian tradition—faith, hope and love—as the guide. I pair them with three practices that they shape and that in turn shape them: education, worship and hospitality. I believe that if we will commit ourselves to recovering these virtues and practices, God will be faithful and we will live in the righteousness, peace and joy of the kingdom (Rom 14:17).

Some hard work lies ahead. Although our culture is turning increasingly to the language of virtue, most of us in the church have not done much critical thinking about virtue ethics in relation to the gospel. Our ethics have been shaped by traditions other than the virtue tradition and, tragically, often by traditions other than the gospel. Although we are cultural beings, we tend to take our culture for granted. Culture is to humans as water is to fish. Someone has said, "If you want to know about water, don't ask a fish." Similarly, we humans are often oblivious to the culture that shapes our lives.

Yet in spite of the difficulties, the time is right for us to consider virtue ethics and our cultural situation. As we see the rise of virtue ethics in our culture, we must think carefully about the relation between virtue ethics and the gospel. As we go through a time of cultural transition, we must examine the ways in which our witness to the gospel is tied to a fading culture and prepare for the challenges and opportunities of a new culture.

In chapter one I examine the rising popularity of virtue ethics. I identify the reasons for its popularity in relation to our dissatisfaction with our culture's previous ethical traditions. At the same time, I identify some dangers to the gospel in the tradition of virtue ethics.

I continue this examination in chapter two by considering some theological objections to virtue ethics. My consideration of these objections gives me an opportunity to transform virtue ethics in light of the claims of the gospel. At the same time I also show how a gospel-shaped ethic of virtue can serve as a guide to Christian faithfulness.

At the end of chapter two I describe the plan of the rest of the book and briefly describe the two terms—*modernity* and *postmodernity*—that I will use throughout the book to identify our cultural situation. What I mean by these terms will become clear as I develop my argument. My use of the terms may raise questions in your mind. Am I a modernist? Am I a postmodernist? Although I am convinced that the culture of modernity is fading and another culture—for the moment called *postmodernity*—is rising, I have no stake in either culture or any other. To the extent that I believe *postmodern* accurately describes our cultural situation, I seek to write theology in a postmodern context. But I do not write as a modern or postmodern theologian. I write as an evangelical theologian concerned for faithful witness to the gospel in every culture.

In chapters three through eight I pair the virtues of faith, hope and love with the practices of education, worship and hospitality. Throughout these chapters I also identify characteristics of our cultural situation that present dangers to and opportunities for witness to the gospel.

In chapter three I give an account of the virtue of faith as a guide to Christian knowing in the midst of both arrogance and skepticism about our ability to know. I consider especially the division between faith and knowledge and our connection of faith with uncertainty and knowledge with certainty. I argue that the virtue of faith that is shaped by the gospel teaches us the opposite—that the only true and certain way of knowing is by faith.

In chapter four I describe how the virtue of faith and Christian knowing forms, and is formed by, the practice of education. This practice is not something confined to a classroom. Rather, it pervades our lives. So we must be wary of the ways that our culture educates us away from, instead of into, faith.

In chapter five I describe the virtue of hope that guides the Christian way of being in a world marked by a quest for human mastery of our destiny and a descent into despair of such mastery. Here I argue that we must abandon both the illusion of hope built on human powers and the cynical, despairing descent into interminable conflict, in favor of the hope of the gospel. In the gospel our destiny is revealed as something given to us in Christ, not achieved by human effort. Hope is the virtue that witnesses to our destiny—our destination—in God's eschatological redemption.

In chapter six I describe worship as a practice that sustains, and is sustained by, the virtue of hope and our way of being in the world. This practice is not a means of achieving the dreams and desires that we are taught by our culture. Rather, worship is a practice that corrects our vision and thus enables us to see and desire the destiny of the world that has been revealed in the gospel.

In chapter seven I describe the virtue of love as the Christian way of doing in a world marked by the thirst for power and the mastery of others and of the world. Love is not the Christian way of getting and exercising power, it is the Christian way of giving ourselves for the sake of the gospel. Love is not the occasion for others to rule over us, it is the occasion for us to witness to the gospel. Such witness is possible only if we know that God loves us and that our life is secure in Christ.

In chapter eight I describe the practice of hospitality as a means by which we are habituated in love. At the same time, I show that when it is formed by God's love, this much-neglected and trivialized practice actually lies at the heart of the gospel.

In the conclusion I first describe how these virtues and practices intertwine with and reinforce each other. I then return to the central concern of *Gospel Virtues* and call for a recovery of Christian living formed by these virtues and practices as faithful witness to the gospel of Jesus Christ.

One

THE RISING
POPULARITY
OF VIRTUE

. . . .

WHEN WE EVALUATE POLITICIANS, SHOULD WE BE CONCERNED only with their policies, or should we also be concerned about their character? Is morality only about the actions of individuals, or is it also a matter of the kind of community in which we live? What kinds of people are capable of morality? What is the purpose, the goal, of morality?

These are the questions that are being forced upon us by increasing attention to virtue and character. Although "virtue ethics," or "character ethics," has a long tradition, our culture has been largely formed by other approaches to morality that typically are concerned either with our duty in a particular situation or with the consequences of some particular action. With the rising popularity of virtue ethics, those familiar ethical traditions are being increasingly scrutinized.

In popular culture this renewed attention to virtue ethics is evident in the success of William Bennett's works *The Book of Virtues* and *The Moral Compass* and in Hillary Rodham Clinton's book *It Takes a Village*. This attention to the virtues is also reflected in the church: a recent catalog for a Christian book club devoted an entire page to Christian books on the virtues.

At the same time, many of our political debates have been concerned with character. We are no longer concerned solely with public policies and social issues. Now we also consider the character of politicians in our political conflicts. This concern with character represents another way to express the tradition of virtue ethics.

This popular concern for virtues and character has been preceded for many years by renewed attention to virtue in philosophical and theological ethics. Among many philosophical works, one of the most influential is Alasdair MacIntyre's *After Virtue*, which ignited a lively debate. Among theological works, Stanley Hauerwas's *Character and the Christian Life* stands at the head of numerous recent works.[1] These and other philosophical and theological works provide us with rich resources for renewed attention to the virtues in our lives together.

Virtue Ethics—Danger and Opportunity

This turn to questions of virtue and character represents the recognition of failure in our ethical traditions and of the breaking down of morality in our culture. Of course, the virtues and attention to the virtues have never been entirely absent from our culture, but the attention that virtue is now receiving has proven attractive to Christians. This attraction is natural because Christians are deeply concerned about morality.

At the same time, we Christians must also be discerning in our adoption of virtue ethics. The virtues come in many different shapes and sizes—what counts as a virtue in one culture or social setting may not count as a virtue in another. One of the most influential accounts of virtues is Aristotle's *Nicomachean Ethics*, but, as many have pointed out, Aristotle's account is incompatible with Christianity.[2] For instance, Aristotle has no place for the virtue of humility, and his account of friendship precludes the possibility of friendship between God and humanity.

Any account of the virtues depends on particular convictions about what constitutes "the good life," what kind of community forms and is formed by the virtues, what kinds of activities (practices) are involved in the virtues and what tradition we are seeking to sustain by the practice of the virtues we commend. In the midst of the present revival of virtue ethics Christians must exercise vigilance to discern what is required by faithfulness to the gospel.

Nevertheless, as I commend vigilance, I also believe that we have much to learn from virtue ethics. The turn to virtue in our culture also represents an opportunity for the church to witness to the gospel. As we analyze and criticize virtue ethics in light of the gospel, we also want to learn from virtue ethics to see more clearly how to practice the gospel as faithful witnesses in our culture.

Evangelical theology has been rightly wary of some aspects of virtue ethics. Evangelical theology, being rooted in the doctrine of justification by grace through faith, has asserted that virtue ethics undercuts grace. It sees virtue ethics as placing too much within the power of humanity and as verging on salvation as a human achievement—the ancient heresy of Pelagianism.

Though I believe that these criticisms have merit, I also think they can be overcome by giving an account of virtues, rooted in the gospel, that enable us to live faithfully. Therefore I will analyze the rising popularity of virtue ethics and indicate the dangers and opportunities presented by virtue ethics. In the next chapter I will consider some theological concerns about virtue ethics and show how virtue ethics, "Christianly considered," enables faithful witness to the gospel.

Why Virtue Ethics Is Popular

The increasing interest in virtue ethics in our culture comes after a lengthy period during which virtue ethics was relatively neglected. As Gilbert Meilaender suggests, the return to an ethic of virtue signals "a widespread dissatisfaction with an understanding of the moral life which focuses primarily on duties, obligations, troubling moral dilemmas, and borderline cases."[3]

Duties, obligations, troubling moral dilemmas and borderline cases represent the standard understanding of ethics in our culture—people think of ethics as having to do with hard cases. For example, should a person sheltering Jews in her attic during World War II lie to the Nazis in order to protect them? Should I embezzle money to pay for an operation that will save my daughter's life? People have usually dealt with such issues by considering what duty requires or what outcome they want from a particular situation.[4]

Virtue ethics, as I will discuss it here, does not represent something added to these approaches—that is, it does not say that we should add a consideration of virtue to our deliberations about duty, obligation or consequences. Rather, virtue reconceives the whole understanding of ethics and morality. To demonstrate how an ethic of virtue does this, I will examine in some detail the reasons for the increasing dissatisfaction with "traditional" approaches and the rising popularity of virtue ethics.[5] This examination will reveal that an ethic of virtue emphasizes *being* rather than *doing,* that it connects who we are with an overall vision of life and that it makes communities not individuals central to morality.

Although I will be concerned primarily with general cultural trends, keep in mind that by its very nature virtue ethics cannot provide a generic account of the virtues. Any account of the virtues is tied to a particular understanding of who we are, what life is meant to be and what kind of community we aspire to be. One very real danger to the church in the revival of virtue ethics is that in our enthusiasm we will uncritically adopt a virtue ethic that is at odds with our deepest calling and convictions.[6] Therefore as we examine the rising popularity of virtue ethics, we will also consider how our commitment to the gospel reconceives an ethic of virtue.

Dissatisfaction with "decisionism." One of the primary areas of dissatisfaction with "traditional" approaches to ethics is its emphasis on what we might call *decisionism*. Decisionism identifies the tendency of our thinking about ethics toward focusing on discrete decisions. Typically these decisions concern specific situations that reflect a dilemma, such as lying to the Nazis or handing over the Jews who are hiding in my attic. This approach to ethics is unsatisfactory for at least two reasons.[7]

First, decisionism obscures the kind of person an individual must be in order to act morally. Decisionism assumes that anyone, told what is the right thing to do, is capable of doing it. Thus doing the good or right thing in a particular situation does not depend on my character or, in the example above, on my prior history of truth-telling. Rather, morality is concerned with discrete, disconnected acts.

This approach is similar to assuming that, without any prior training, I can run a hundred-yard dash in ten seconds if I am properly instructed in how to do it. But that assumption ignores the ability and training that makes a world-class athlete capable of such feats. Likewise, decisionism ignores the kind of training and history that makes a person capable of doing good.

Second, decisionism tends to treat ethics as a discipline of thinking that is restricted to a special and distinct sphere of living. Morality is practiced well or badly in the midst of dilemmas and crises. Thus ethics has to do only with a restricted area of life in which we only occasionally engage. In other words, the decisionist focus of "traditional" ethics is on the big events in life. It neglects everyday living as the proper concern of ethics. For example, a decisionist emphasis in ethics might lead a member of a hospital ethics committee to describe the committee's work as deliberating on situations where "values" are in conflict. This is an unsatisfactory way of thinking about ethics because it ignores other questions that are properly ethical, such as how a hospital treats patients routinely. To take another example, decisionism might lead a supervisor to think that she is being moral because she does not embezzle, even though at the same time she daily treats employees with disrespect.

In contrast to these weaknesses of our usual ways of thinking about morality, an ethic of virtue places an emphasis on the kind of people we must be to be moral. It also turns our moral attention to the whole of life rather than to some restricted, special sphere that concerns only an occasional decision in the midst of a dilemma. Virtue ethics recognizes that morality is concerned with the particular kind of people we are, the character that we have cultivated. An ethics of virtue is not merely an alternative way of resolving dilemmas or making decisions. Should one lie to Nazis in order to save Jews? The concern of a virtue ethic would not be with this dilemma but with the character of the people who sheltered Jews. What virtues marked those people—courage, justice, compassion? What kind of community cultivated and sustained those virtues? What vision of life compelled such action?[8] By telling the story of those who sheltered Jews and by analyzing and expositing the virtues, community and vision of life that marked them, an ethic of virtue seeks to train people in morality.

Thus an ethic of virtue does not teach that we can be moral simply by being given a rule to follow or by deciding what to do in a particular instance. Rather, virtue ethics recognizes that we must be trained in the moral life. Just as an athlete who aspires to Olympic glory begins with small steps toward her goal, so also people who aspire to be mature moral persons begin with small steps. Perseverance and faithfulness in small matters develop in us the moral ability to be faithful in larger matters. But even this way of putting it is misleading, because for most of us faithfulness in small matters is the largest moral challenge we will face.

In addition to turning our attention to the ethical training of the whole person, an ethic of virtue enlarges our vision of the moral. No longer is morality restricted to a narrow sphere of life. Since an ethic of virtue is concerned with who we are and not just with our specific actions and restricted areas of life, all areas of life are equally the concern of moral persons. Every area of life contributes something to the kind of people we are. How we treat a store clerk is as much a moral matter as is our not shoplifting. How often we drive our cars in an energy-scarce world is as much a moral matter as is our not drinking and driving.

The gospel, virtue ethics and decisionism. No matter how hard I might train, the limitations of my physique preclude my becoming an Olympic-caliber shot-putter. Even many who might have the physical qualifications to be a world-class athlete are prevented from being such by their circumstances—they lack the nutrition, the financial support or other things required to develop their abilities. An ethic of virtue provides an attractive alternative to the decisionism of "traditional" ethics, but it also raises some questions for the Christian.

These kinds of concerns have long marked the tradition of virtue ethics. For instance, Aristotle believed that slaves and women could not develop the virtues that he commends in the *Nicomachean Ethics.* Slaves could not do so because they lacked the opportunity. Women could not do so because they lacked the natural ability. Moreover, others who may be capable of becoming virtuous are born into families and social contexts that do not train them in the tradition of the virtues.

Although we should not downplay the subtle ways that we exclude some from moral possibilities, the breakdown of familial and social structures in today's culture is probably the most obvious.[9] If we stand within a culture that has long neglected training in virtue, how can we begin to recover a virtue ethic? In this context, the gospel of Jesus Christ has much to contribute through its revelation of God's grace.

For the Christian, God's grace is always present as a power that transcends our particular situation and personal history. As I will argue in the next chapter, our recognition of grace does not preclude training in grace, but it does properly locate the power of goodness in God. In a sense, the presence of grace in our lives promises us that we can all become moral Olympians, not in our own strength but in the power of the Holy Spirit.[10]

In like manner, our recognition of grace does not downplay the significance of a community that trains us in virtues, but it does tell us the source and kind of community that teaches us goodness.[11] Even if that community is absent today, we need not despair, for the grace of God is present for the renewal of the church.

Unlike virtue ethics, which makes all of life the arena of morality, the gospel teaches that life is a seamless whole under the lordship of Jesus Christ. Thus any Christian account of virtues must keep central not questions of morality but questions of discipleship. Christians may use the language of morality—the language of virtues, of goodness and the like—but that language must always be reoriented, transformed, redeemed, by the gospel of Jesus Christ.[12]

This last point is particularly important, because no account of the virtues is independent of a community and a particular vision of life. The virtues needed to sustain a Greek warrior-state were different from those required to maintain a modern nation-state in the midst of the Cold War or an advanced capitalist society at the end of the twentieth century. Still different virtues are needed to sustain the community of disciples of Jesus Christ as faithful witnesses to the gospel. The gospel itself provides Christians with the virtues needed for faithful living.

In relation to the decisionism of "traditional" ethics, an ethic of virtue turns our attention from discrete, disconnected acts to the training and character that we reveal in our lives, from a narrow sphere of morality to the whole of life as morally engaged.

In relation to virtue ethics the gospel of Jesus Christ teaches that the virtues are marks of God's grace in disciples of Jesus Christ, not of mere human effort, and the gospel reveals all of life as under the lordship of Jesus Christ.

Dissatisfaction with the "priority of the right." Another area of rising dissatisfaction with ethics is the priority of the "right" to the "good." In most of our talk about ethics we are used to thinking about what is the right thing to do. This way of thinking and talking so pervades our culture that we have great difficulty avoiding it. Whenever we begin thinking ethically, we "naturally" ask what is "right." But this seems natural only because our culture has taught us to think in this way. For excellent reasons, however, we are beginning to question the priority of the right and turning to the "good" of virtue ethics.

In "traditional" ethics the priority of the right to the good signifies an attempt to overcome the conflict inherent in opposing accounts of the good. As Alasdair MacIntyre has shown, prior to the Enlightenment ethics depended on a threefold scheme: human beings as we are, human beings as we should be and how humans can get from where (or how) we are to where (or how) we should be.[13] The language of "where we should be" was a vision of life, a view of what is "good" for humans. How to get from where we are to where we should be was the account of morality as the means to accomplish this task. But because different communities gave different accounts of where we should be, conflict, even violent confrontation, arose. In response to this violence, society, under the tutelage of various thinkers, abandoned any talk about what is good for humans. So people were left with accounts of where humans are and accounts of morality—"what we should do." When people were told how they should act morally and then asked why they should act in that way, they could no longer say, "So you can fulfill this vision of the life that is good for humans." They could only say, "Because it is right." But as MacIntyre also shows, what is right to do only makes sense if it is connected to some vision of the good. As a result of our unwillingness or inability to make that connection, morality becomes incoherent. Morality becomes, eventually, merely a matter of individual choice and preference.[14]

In our culture we are becoming increasingly dissatisfied with the consequences of the priority of the right to the good.[15] Of course, even the "traditional" emphasis on the right incorporated a covert notion of the good. It might be expressed something like this: the good life for human beings is one spent not interfering with others' morality and not holding any convictions that would lead us to kill others. Yet the twentieth century bears bloody witness to the failure of the "priority of the right" to end humanity's violence. Moreover, the recent history of our culture testifies to the inability of the right to sustain a morality that is worthy of the name.

In the midst of this radical failure and dissatisfaction, an ethic of virtue offers great hope: perhaps what we need in order to regain our moral compass is a renewed conception of what is good for humans. We can see around us signs of this hope. Many are offering new accounts of the good. These accounts seek to find or build some consensus in society about what is good for humans. Some of them draw on our common civic identity in order to seek some agreement about the good.[16] Others seek to revive the "traditional" account by reorienting it around a conception of the good.[17]

In these accounts people are seeking to describe a vision of the good that morality enables us to realize. These are not merely accounts of "the good life," as we use the phrase today, but are an effort to identify the purpose, the goal, the destiny of human life. In virtue ethics then our morality is teleological—that is, the way we live is shaped by our convictions about where our life is headed.

The gospel, virtue ethics and the priority of the right. In light of the fragmentation of our society, we can understand the appeal of an ethic oriented toward the good and the attraction of these attempts to promote a conception of the good. However, for a Christian none of these accounts goes far enough. The gospel reveals that the good of humanity is not found in any human institution but is given in the kingdom of God. This conviction relativizes all other accounts of the good and brings all human loyalties under the lordship of Jesus Christ.

As I will argue in later chapters, the fact that this "good" is a gift from God calls forth a set of virtues very different from other accounts. Moreover, this gift of the good creates a people who recognize that their warfare is not with "blood and flesh" but with "the spiritual forces of evil in the heavenly places" (see Eph 6:10-20, esp. v. 12). The way this good was given—through the life, death and resurrection of Jesus Christ—provides Christians with a model: living by the enabling power of the Spirit. In the face of the failure of the good or the right to end human violence, the kingdom of God is the good that is worth dying for but for which a person cannot kill because that would be to orient life to a different good. One of the tragedies of history is that those who claim the name of Christ have been so captive to other goods that they have been willing to kill in the name of Christ.[18]

So in contrast to the priority of the right in "traditional" accounts of morality, an ethic of virtue gives priority to the good. By so doing, virtue ethics seeks to restore the coherence of morality by providing it with a teleology (a purpose, an end, a goal). In relation to virtue ethics the gospel reveals the teleology of humanity—indeed, of all creation—in the kingdom of God. This good is not the end of humanity that we typically envision, nor is it achieved by humanity. It is the loving gift of God in Jesus Christ.

Dissatisfaction with individualism. In addition to dissatisfaction with decisionism and the priority of the right in "traditional" ethics, our culture is also turning away from individualism to community.[19] This individualism is a concomitant of decisionism

28 *Gospel Virtues*

and the priority given to the right. If ethics is primarily concerned with decisions—that is, if morality is primarily a matter of discrete acts by persons whose history, whose previous acts, have little or no bearing on the present situation—then no community, no shared history, has any bearing on issues of morality. If community is introduced, its existence is secondary to the individual and its importance lies in its contribution to the fulfillment of the individual.

The individual and his or her acts then become the primary categories for ethical analysis. In this tradition the duty of the individual is first to himself or herself. Although some ethics that emphasize duty have set it within the larger context of duty to a community or to a particular role in a community, individualism has so shaped our culture that one's first duty is to oneself. Or, if the consequences of an act are in view, the issue is what will be the consequence of a particular act for the individual.[20] So, for example, individualism leads an elected political representative to think first about his duty to preserve and extend his power or of the consequences of an act for his own power or reelection chances, not about his duty to his constituency or the consequences of an act for his district.

Likewise, the priority of the right gives rise to individualism by disconnecting our actions from any relation to the good or by serving an implicit good—what is good for humanity is that each individual should be free to seek his or her own good as long as it does not interfere with others' freedom. Thus what is "right" for me is a matter of individual preference. I must simply be careful that what is "right" for me does not impede others' pursuit and achievement of what is right for them. In our culture the ethical slogan is "I can do what I want as long as it doesn't hurt anyone."

Our western European culture is growing increasingly dissatisfied with this kind of individualism. We are discovering that it vitiates moral judgment on many important matters, that even if it does not persuade a majority its reasoning can be used to "justify" practices that most of us find reprehensible. We are discovering that, at its worst, the tendencies of individualism result in morality as simply the exercise of power. What is moral is determined by what a person can get away with.

In the midst of this kind of individualism, our culture is turning increasingly to an emphasis on community. An ethic of virtue proves attractive in this situation because virtue ethics relies on the life of a community for forming the virtuous life. Virtue takes training, and that training takes place within a particular community. But here is precisely the challenge: *which* community are we talking about? The virtues that we advocate depend on the kind of community we seek or in which we live. For example, a terrorist cell is a tightly knit community that requires the cultivation of particular "virtues." The virtues required to sustain a dictatorship are different from the virtues required to sustain a democracy. Likewise, the virtues required to resist a dictator or a democracy are different. The virtues of thrift, self-discipline and generosity sustain one kind of economic community. The virtues of greed, self-indulgence and profligacy sustain another kind. To which community are we turning?

The gospel, virtue ethics and individualism. In this uncertainty we the church face tremendous opportunity and challenge. The challenge is not to be so overwhelmed by the breakdown of our society that we simply adopt whatever vision of community promises the greatest hope of rebuilding society. MacIntyre has persuasively argued that an ethics of virtue will only be recovered if we shun any attempt to shore up or restore the social order.[21] But although MacIntyre makes a cryptic reference to "another— doubtless very different—St. Benedict," he does not specify which community or which virtues he is commending.[22] Here we Christians must adduce the church as that community called forth by God as witness to the gospel of Jesus Christ. It is *this* community and *this* task that call us to particular virtues required to sustain the church and its witness to the gospel.

At this point, the Christian turn to the church and the gospel also meets one of the criticisms that MacIntyre and others have faced—that of succumbing to the "sectarian temptation." This temptation may take many forms, but here the accusation is that the good of others is neglected so that my own little group may prosper. Thus when MacIntyre urges us not to "save" the social order but to gather in small communities of virtue, he seems to some to be commending a kind of group selfishness. This communal selfishness says that as long as the virtues are prospering in my little group, what is happening in the rest of society does not matter.

Whether or not MacIntyre succumbs to this temptation does not concern me here. What does concern me is that the turn to the church and the gospel, as I describe it, is far from succumbing to any supposed sectarian temptation. Indeed, my turning to the gospel virtues is rooted in the conviction that the only hope of the world is the gospel and that the only hope of faithfulness to the gospel on the part of the church is for it to be the church and cultivate the virtues that sustain the life of witness.

This call to the life of the church enables us to resist one of the great dangers in the turn to virtue ethics. In the context of the powerful individualism of our culture, virtue may easily become merely another means of achieving my own fulfillment. Gilbert Meilaender, a theologian who advocates a recovery of virtue ethics, notes the danger here of "the 'fat, relentless ego.' " As Meilaender notes, what God calls for in the gospel is "not just discipline [of the ego] but rebirth."[23] Later he warns that an emphasis on virtue may lead to self-regard and self-centeredness: "Does not the very language of virtue suggest too much concentration upon the self, too intense a devotion to self-cultivation?"[24] In other words, in our individualistic culture, will not many people hear *virtue* as simply another and better means to get what they want, to achieve self-fulfillment?

Here the gospel calls us to conversion from ourselves to God and disciplines us toward a good greater than ourselves. Here, because our lives are "hidden with Christ in God" (Col 3:3) and because Christ gave up his life for others, we are called to a higher righteousness (vv. 5-17) and enabled by the Spirit of God to witness to that life. With Meilaender's warnings in mind, I will seek in this book to give an account of three virtues of the Christian life—faith, hope and love—that reflect this call of the gospel.

Conclusion

I have introduced some aspects of an ethic of virtue by analyzing the appeal of virtue ethics in light of dissatisfaction with three developments in our culture's ethical tradition. The appeal of virtue ethics should be clear but so also should be some of the thinking Christians must do if they are to live out the gospel in the midst of these changes. This situation is an opportunity for the church to strengthen its life and witness to the gospel by learning from the tradition of the virtues. To develop this claim further, I must consider in chapter two some theological objections to the Christian use of an ethic of virtue and lay the foundation for a gospel-centered account of the virtues.

Two

CAN VIRTUE
BE CHRISTIAN?

••••••••••••••••••••••

THE RISING POPULARITY OF VIRTUE ETHICS REPRESENTS SOME DIS-satisfaction with our culture's ethical tradition and with the current state of morality. This dissatisfaction is something with which Christians may sympathize, but is the turn to virtue ethics something that Christians should support? The question is not so easily answered as asked because there is no one thing called *virtue ethics*. The various accounts of the virtues are rooted in particular visions of the good, shaping particular kinds of communities and advocating a particular set of virtues.

As Christians we have no stake in defending the notion of virtue or the practice of ethics. What concerns us is the vitality of Christian living and the faithfulness of Christian witness to the gospel. I believe that virtue ethics provides us with some resources for thinking about the Christian life and that the turn to virtue ethics provides the church with an opportunity for renewed witness to the gospel in a culture that is increasingly post-Christian.

Numerous theologians in the Christian tradition have made use of the language of virtue to describe the Christian life.[1] This tradition provides a rich resource for us contemporary Christians, but as we face the challenges of our own cultural situation we need to consider anew the virtues and practices that will enable our faithful witness to the gospel.

In this chapter my ultimate goal is to present a framework within which we may use the tradition of virtue ethics to enable more faithful Christian living. I will first consider several theological objections to virtue ethics and take these objections seriously as markers of pitfalls that we must avoid. At the same time, however, I will argue that if virtue ethics is appropriately transformed by the gospel, then an account of virtues and practices embodied by the gospel may guide our recovery of faithful witness. Then I will consider, in light of the gospel, Alasdair MacIntyre's outline of the elements of an ethic of virtue. This will give us the framework within which my account will be set. Finally I will briefly identify the three virtues and three practices that we will consider in the following chapters.

Theological Objections to Virtue Ethics

A number of theologians have raised significant objections to virtue ethics. Although my concern is with the vitality of Christian living and the witness of the church to the gospel and not with the defense of virtue ethics, I believe that an examination of virtue ethics in light of the gospel will help us to be more faithful in our witness. Therefore as we consider these objections to virtue ethics I will seek to show how these objections may be met by a virtue ethics that is transformed by the gospel.

The theological denial of ethics. The first objection to virtue ethics is a comprehensive "theological denial of ethics." Karl Barth is a prime example. In his *Church Dogmatics* Barth denies the validity of ethics independent of dogmatics.[2] Note, however, that Barth's denial of ethics is not a blanket one. Rather, out of his commitment to affirming the sovereignty and grace of God, Barth denies that any valid ethics can be developed from another source.[3] Similarly Dietrich Bonhoeffer's *Ethics* begins with the assertion that Christian ethics must call into question all other forms of ethics that seek "knowledge of good and evil." In so doing Christian theology sets the concerns of ethics in an entirely new context—the work of God in Christ.[4] Finally Donald Bloesch asserts that "what constitutes the Christian life is not morality (as the world understands this) but faith and its fruits."[5]

Together these theologians offer salutary warnings as prefaces to their own ethical reflection. Of course, after giving these warnings each goes on to develop his own particular Christian ethics. Taking heed of their warnings, I will do the same. Christian ethics, while recognizing that God's grace is sovereign, gives an account of the *work* of grace. Christian ethics, though recognizing that God is the source of goodness, gives an account of how that goodness takes shape *in* human lives. Christian ethics exposes the illusory goods toward which we orient our lives and directs us toward that good (*telos,* to use the language of virtue ethics) revealed in Jesus Christ and describes for us the particular form of faith and its fruits in our time.

So the theological denial of ethics warns us against the human propensity for self-justification and the denial of our need for God's grace. These dangers are particularly acute in the practice of ethics, so I take them as stringent admonitions to be heeded in my own work. At the same time, my reflection on these warnings gives me guidance for the practice of ethics that is peculiarly Christian.

Graces, not virtues. A second theological objection pertains more directly to the approach that I am taking. It argues that we should speak more of graces than of virtues. Virtues indicate the unfolding of human potentialities, whereas graces are the manifestations of the work of the Holy Spirit within us. It is not the fulfillment of human powers but the transformation of the human heart that is the emphasis in an authentically evangelical ethics.[6]

While providing a Christian account of virtue ethics and some Christian virtues, Meilaender warns that

before Christian ethicists latch too quickly onto an ethic of virtue, it is important to remember that an emphasis on character may sit uneasily with some strands of Christian belief. . . . A sketch of the virtues is a picture of a fulfilled life, of the successful realization of a self. Such an approach cannot without difficulty be incorporated into a vision of the world which has at its center a crucified God—which takes, that is, not self-realization but self-sacrifice as its central theme. Furthermore, the very notion of character seems to suggest . . . habitual behavior, abilities within our power, an acquired possession. And this in turn may be difficult to reconcile with the Christian emphasis on grace, the sense of the sinner's constant need of forgiveness, and the belief that we can have no claims upon the freedom of God.[7]

Together these lengthy quotes present a serious theological problem: Does not the language of virtue emphasize human ability and achievement to the detriment of the grace of God, downplaying or even denying human sinfulness and our need for forgiveness? Their warnings of the dangers of virtue language in Christian ethics is well taken.

In my account of the Christian virtues of faith, hope and love, and the practices of education, worship and hospitality, I will constantly build on the foundation of God's grace, be aware of human sinfulness and our need of forgiveness, and recognize that only the work of the Spirit in our lives enables the Christian life.[8] At the same time, I believe that speaking of Christian *virtue* directs us toward the habitual patterns of the Christian life—enabled by God's grace through the Holy Spirit, to be sure—that witness to the gospel. Likewise, speaking of *practices* directs the church toward the kind of community that embodies and forms these virtues.

Heroic virtue and Christian virtue. In a thorough and profound account John Milbank provides a theological critique of virtue ethics that also enables us to reconceive, in light of the gospel, both the notion of virtue and the particular virtues. Milbank's account is both a comprehensive deconstruction of non-Christian accounts of virtue ethics and a profound reconstruction of a Christian version of virtue. I will not try to reproduce his argument here, but by drawing out some details I will identify the aspects of his argument that will guide my account.[9]

The most comprehensive contrast that Milbank draws between a Christian concept of virtue and the concept of virtue in "antique" ethics and various retrievals of "antique" ethics is the contrast between nonheroic and heroic virtue. Indeed, according to Milbank this difference is so great that "Christian virtue is no longer exactly virtue" (p. 369).

As Milbank shows, the heroic conception of virtue to the Greeks and others presupposes the finality of conflict *(agōn)* and violence. In this conflict humanity is on its own or in contest with the gods, and virtue is viewed as a victory accomplished through human effort. As a result, an ethic of heroic virtue is no ethic at all because it has no real concept of the good.[10]

In contrast, the nonheroic conception of virtue proper to Christianity views virtue as a gift of God and presupposes *"the ontological priority of peace to conflict"* (p. 363). That is, rooted in the grace of God through the atonement of Jesus Christ, Christianity envisions peace as the end, or "good," of creation. Thus *"only* Christianity, once it has arrived, really appears ethical at all" (p. 362).

Milbank's critique of virtue penetrates more deeply than the objections of Bloesch and Meilaender by exposing the fundamental reason that an ethic of virtue tends to denigrate or deny God's grace and elevate human achievement. More important, Milbank shows that a Christian ethic of virtue is rooted in an understanding of reality very different from other ethics of virtue.

Against the heroic view of this world as a place of interminable conflict, the gospel reveals the world to be reconciled to God through the sacrifice of Jesus Christ.[11] Instead of virtue being the means by which we grow in the power to conquer all threats, virtue becomes our habituation in the life of peace made possible by Jesus Christ.[12]

Milbank's insight into this fundamental difference of Christian virtue will guide us in the following chapters. Milbank exposes the fundamental difference made when we direct an account of the virtues and practices toward faithful witness to the gospel. Any account of virtue rooted in the Christian gospel must be directed by peace, not endless conflict.[13] Virtue is not what humans achieve but what God enables. Given this conception of virtue, the specific virtues—and the account of those virtues—will be different for the Christian.

Intertwined with his Christian reconception of virtue, Milbank also directs us toward some specific content for a Christian ethic of virtue. Most important is the difference between Aristotle and Aquinas about what makes "virtue really and not accidentally virtuous" (p. 360). For Aristotle, what makes virtue virtuous is *prudentia* or *phronēsis*. For Aquinas, what makes virtue virtuous is charity.[14] This difference is profound, since for Aristotle an intellectual virtue makes virtue really virtue, whereas for Aquinas charity—a virtue entirely lacking in Aristotle—is the very form of the virtues. This emphasis on charity, or love, is rooted in the gospel and transforms the whole tradition of the virtues.

Divine command ethics, not virtue ethics. One more theological objection to Christian virtue ethics needs to be considered. This objection argues that the primary biblical language for the Christian life is obedience to divine commands rather than the development of virtue.

This debate over command and virtue as the proper language for Christian life involves a number of issues. Some of these I considered in my examination of the rising popularity of virtue ethics, and others are not relevant to our topic.[15] However, at first glance this objection appears serious since it draws on the biblical language of command. Certainly much of the language of Scripture is in the imperative. Nevertheless I believe that the language and concepts of virtue ethics are, at least in our present circumstances, superior to the language of divine command for several reasons.[16]

First, virtue ethics is superior to divine command ethics because it directs our attention to the kind of person that perceives and obeys God's commands. Certainly by God's grace we can hear and obey God's command in a moment. But is it not also likely that a person who has previously obeyed God, who has a history of obedience to God, will be more likely to hear and obey? This history, this continuity of character, is that toward which virtue ethics directs our attention. Moreover, the biblical imperative always presupposes the indicative—the prior history of God's grace in our lives that habituates us in obedience.

Second, virtue ethics directs our attention toward the biblical emphasis on growth in the Christian life. Paul's imagery of the fruit of the Spirit and his and Peter's explicit references to virtues (Gal 5:22-23; Phil 4:8; 2 Pet 1:5) emphasize growth and habituation in the Christian life. Likewise, Paul's call to "put away" the old way of life and "clothe yourselves with" the new life in Christ describes habitual ways of living that involve growth (Eph 4:22-24; compare Col 3:5-11). Finally the biblical teaching that through Christ we enter into friendship with God teaches us that we are to mature in the Christian life, that we are not to remain babes who always require a direct command from a parent in order to act.[17]

Nothing that I have argued here excludes from Christian virtue ethics a concern for God's commands. Indeed, any ethic that is grounded in Scripture must attend to God's commands. Also, nothing that I have argued precludes a divine command morality from incorporating these same concerns.[18] Nevertheless, in our present circumstances the language and concepts of virtue ethics provide us with the best tools for articulating the Christian life.

At the same time, as I have already noted, an ethics of virtue must be transformed by the gospel.

The Gospel and Virtue Ethics

Up to this point we have been gradually entering into the world of virtue ethics by considering the reasons for the rise of virtue ethics and some theological concerns with virtue ethics. Along the way I have been indicating some changes that the gospel would make in an ethic of virtue and some insights into the Christian life that we gain from virtue ethics. Now I need to bring these elements together to present a more systematic case for a Christian virtue ethics.[19]

In *After Virtue* Alasdair MacIntyre identifies five elements of an ethics of virtue.[20] An explication of these five elements, drawing on my previous analysis, will provide a sketch of the ethics of virtue that I will partially develop in the following chapters, but I will not be bound to MacIntyre's account. I am simply going to use MacIntyre's five elements and give my own account of them in light of the gospel. Further, I will not be developing directly all five elements in the following chapters. My focus will be on two of them: virtues and practices. Nevertheless the other elements are necessary to my account, for various understandings of them underlie my account of the virtues and practices. Therefore I give this outline of them in order to indicate the fuller context within which the virtues and practices come to life.

My purpose here is not so much to provide an ethics of virtue as to provide an account of the Christian way of life in these times. Consequently there are a number of controversies in virtue ethics to which I will allude but not address at length.

A living tradition. A Christian ethic of virtue must be developed within the context of the living tradition of the gospel. *Living tradition* is MacIntyre's term. A better, biblical description might be that the gospel is the "everlasting reality" of God's work in Jesus Christ.[21]

As the everlasting reality, the gospel has a past, present and future. Its past is rooted in the preparation for the gospel in the Old Testament and in the embodiment of the gospel in the coming of Jesus Christ. It is the continuing reality in the present because Jesus Christ has risen and is present through the Holy Spirit. To put it colloquially, Jesus Christ did not retire to heaven after his resurrection—he continues to work in the world even today.[22] The gospel also has a future—the work of God revealed in the gospel is not yet complete. On the basis of this past, present and future of the gospel we may say several things about a Christian virtue ethics.

First, since the Old and New Testaments bear witness to the gospel, our ethics depends on their witness. Moreover, since their witness is foundational and Spirit-inspired, they are our primary authority.[23] However, we cannot simply read out of Scripture rules or principles for the Christian life. Rather, since Christ is present today, when we speak of Christian ethics as an account of the Christian way of life we are seeking to describe how "the form of Jesus Christ itself works upon us in such a manner that it moulds our form into its own likeness (Gal 4:19)."[24] These sentences describe a more complex view of the role and authority of Scripture in Christian ethics than some other accounts, but I believe that this view more nearly accords with our actual practice. Two examples—one biblical, another contemporary— may be instructive.

Acts 15 is an account of the early church trying to discern how God is at work among the Gentiles. The Old Testament apparently taught that a man had to be circumcised to be a part of God's covenant, yet Gentiles were receiving the Spirit without having been circumcised. So the Jerusalem Council of Acts 15 sought to discern how Christ was being formed among them in that day and concluded that their traditional reading of Scripture was wrong. Nevertheless the authority of Scripture remained primary for them, since the council concluded with James's quotation of Amos 9 as a guide to what God was doing. This is the "living tradition" of the gospel at work through the presence of the Holy Spirit.

Similarly today many who were staunch allies in developing an account of biblical inerrancy find themselves disagreeing on the biblical teaching about the roles of men and women. After working for many years and producing a detailed statement on the inerrancy of Scripture, the members of the International Council on Biblical Inerrancy found that their statement could not resolve their differences about the roles of men and women.[25] The point here is not that we should despair of developing a biblically grounded Christian ethics. Rather, we must recognize that we are a part of a living tradition that is formed by our very arguments and by the way we engage those arguments.

The everlasting reality of the gospel means that the incarnate, crucified and risen Jesus Christ is being formed in us today by the power of the Holy Spirit.[26] The work of Christian ethics is to discern how that formation is taking place.

The telos *of humanity.* For MacIntyre, virtue ethics is inextricably linked to a person's view of the *telos*—the end, purpose, goal—of humanity. We may also speak of this as the good, or "the good life," for humans. In this way virtue ethics is teleological in its thinking—that is, it always has an end in view and morality is always to be directed toward that end. The gospel reorients this element of virtue ethics in two ways.

First, the gospel teaches us to speak of eschatology rather than teleology. Evangelicals are used to thinking of eschatology in relation to various millennial schemes and questions about Christ's return, the rapture and the tribulation. But in the midst of these questions is a more profound meaning to eschatology— that the end is in God's hand and that its shape has already been revealed in Jesus Christ. Whatever the chronological details of the end, God's purpose is to judge and redeem the world through Jesus Christ. We have seen the future in Jesus Christ. This means that the *telos* of humanity lies ultimately in the work of God, not in human nature as such or in any community created by humanity.

But that does not mean that Christians passively await a future which is in God's hands. Because Jesus Christ, who is the future, is already present and being formed in us through the Holy Spirit, the way we live today must be directed toward that future.[27] That is the very conviction that guided the thinking of Paul, as exemplified in Colossians 3:1-3: "So if you have been raised with Christ, seek the things that are above, where Christ is, seated at the right hand of God. Set your minds on things that are above, not on things that are on earth, for you have died, and your life is hidden with Christ in God" (see also Rom 6).

Second, the *telos*—or better, the eschaton—for Christians is not only for humanity, it is for all creation. God in Christ intends not merely the redemption of humanity but the redemption of all creation. Paul reflects this conviction in his statements that all creation longs for the future glory (Rom 8) and that "in Christ God was reconciling the world to himself" (2 Cor 5:19).

This eschatological vision guards against the egocentric and anthropocentric view of life toward which virtue ethics can so easily drift. This vision directs our lives. If the future of creation, including humanity, has been revealed in Jesus Christ, then we should seek to live today in accord with that future. By the power of the Holy Spirit, that life is a present actuality. A Christian ethic of virtue seeks to direct us toward just such a life.[28]

Community. Any ethic of virtue depends on a particular vision of community. Since I have considered this at some length and since the account of practices in the following chapters will indirectly develop an account of the Christian community, we will only briefly consider this element here.[29] Obviously the community that shapes the Christian virtues is the church. Two characteristics of the church are important to note for Christian virtue ethics.

First, the church does not exist for itself. Just as any account of Christian virtues is ultimately for the sake of witness to the gospel, so also any account of the church as the community of those virtues is ultimately for the sake of its witness to the gospel. This is vital because of the corrupting power of institutions. As MacIntyre shows, virtues and the practices that form them (and are formed by them) depend on and give rise to institutional structures.[30] Yet institutions tend to take on a life of their own. Their acquisitiveness and competitiveness tend to corrupt the very virtues and practices that formed them and that they were meant to sustain. This happens in the church when the life of the church is directed toward sustaining the church rather than sustaining a witness to the gospel.[31]

Second, the church as a community of virtues that witness to the gospel must recognize that it is "set apart."[32] The church is set apart in two ways. *It is set apart to God:* its origin and its continuing life are rooted in the grace of God through the Holy Spirit. *It is set apart from the world:* its virtues and practices are rooted in the gospel, not in the world. The gospel calls the church not to a better life but to a new life, not to morality but to redemption.

With this warning clearly in mind, I can agree with Stanley Hauerwas that since the gospel is the redemption of the world, the witness of the church is for the sake of the world:

> The first social task of the church . . . is to be the church and thus help the world understand itself as world. That world, to be sure, is God's world, God's good creation, which is all the more distorted by sin because it is still bounded by God's goodness. For the church to be the church, therefore, is not anti-world, but rather an attempt to show what the world is meant to be as God's good creation.[33]

Therefore in our current circumstances any account of the church as a community of virtues must resist the strong temptation to provide what the world thinks is needed in the midst of moral fragmentation and breakdown. What the world needs is the gospel; what the church is called to do is to witness to the gospel through the practice of Christian virtues. As the church witnesses to the gospel, it lives for the sake of the world, whose only salvation is the gospel of Jesus Christ.

Practices. In three of the following chapters I will be describing practices of the church that exhibit Christian virtues and that in turn contribute to the further development of those virtues. Here I will offer a preliminary sketch of the importance of practices for Christian virtue ethics.[34]

First, the practices of the church, when they are properly practices, engage the grace of God—that is, practices are not mere human activities. So any account of practices of the church must show clearly how they are dependent on God's grace. Every practice of the church must be explicable as a sign of God's grace. Moreover, every practice of the church must have as its goal deeper participation in the grace of God. Thus, for example, when I seek later to describe education as a practice of the church, I must be careful not to describe it as something that can be conceived apart from God's grace on the basis of human effort alone.

Second, the practices of the church embody and extend Christian virtues. Certainly the virtues may be exhibited apart from practices, but it is the practices that sustain the virtues and school us in what they properly are. Thus, for example, hope is a Christian virtue that should pervade our lives. But worship is a practice of the church that teaches us the basis and form of our hope. Worship warns us against false hope that is built on illusory foundations—idolatry—and directs us toward true hope rooted in the grace of God in Jesus Christ.

Third, the practices of the church have a history. The life of a community and its practices are inextricably linked. That means that the standards for excellence in a practice are not a matter of private judgment. A practice may certainly be modified in the course of its history, but such modification, even when initiated by an individual, is ultimately judged by the community in relation to its "living tradition," its conception of the eschaton and the virtues that it seeks to embody.

Thus the virtue of love and the practice of hospitality, for example, cannot mean whatever we want them to mean in our present circumstances. They do not come to us as empty forms that may be filled with whatever meaning we choose. Rather, love and hospitality come out of a long tradition of reflection and practice that is rooted in the gospel and the wisdom of the church under the guidance of the Holy Spirit. If our love and hospitality are to be Christian, we must submit ourselves to the discipline of this tradition.

Virtues. Any virtue ethics must not concern itself only with virtue, it must also give an account of particular virtues that are consonant with the other elements that we have already described. Since three of the following chapters develop accounts of the theological virtues of faith, hope and love, the discussion here will be brief. Although I could outline some shared characteristics of the virtues in a particular tradition, only a description of particular virtues can give a full account.

The virtues that form our Christians lives must arise from the everlasting reality of the gospel, our convictions about the eschaton and the nature of the church. They must also be inextricably linked to the practices of the church that are formed by the virtues and sustain them. An account of the virtues is a description of how Christ is being formed in us by the Holy Spirit. To turn this around, we may also say that an account of Christian virtues is a description of how we are being conformed to Jesus Christ.

The virtues are the work of God's grace in human lives. Here the emphasis is on the *work* of God's grace. The conviction reflected in this emphasis is not only that God's goodness is the source of human goodness but, further, that God's grace actually makes humans good. Humans are not merely receptacles or conduits of God's goodness. They do not merely do good things occasionally or frequently but are actually being made good by God's grace.

The virtues identify the pattern of our lives that reflects our character. That is, virtues are not merely individual, virtuous acts, nor are they habitual rule-following. Rather, the virtues spring from our innermost being (our "character") as it is renewed and habituated in grace by the Holy Spirit. In this connection the virtues also reveal our beliefs about the nature of reality, about the *telos* (or eschaton) of humanity and all creation.

Finally the many virtues that form the Christian life find their unity in love: "Above all, clothe yourselves with love, which binds everything together in perfect harmony" (Col 3:14). This love is not an empty form that we may fill with our own preferences and desires. It is the story of God's act in Jesus Christ which continues with power in the world today. The Christian virtues describe the ways in which we participate in that story and in which that story is made actual as a witness to others and as an invitation to have that story formed in us.

Conclusion

In this chapter I have examined some theological objections to a Christian ethic of virtue. In so doing I have identified some ways in which any Christian appropriation of virtue ethics would transform that tradition in faithfulness to the gospel. I have also considered a preliminary sketch of a Christian ethic of virtue.

However, a Christian ethic of virtue must go beyond these general reflections on the value and shape of an ethic of virtue to actually proposing an account of (at least some) Christian virtues. This, indeed, is one of the attractions of virtue ethics—it does not exhaust its energy on questions that are preliminary to actually doing ethics. It has traditionally been bold in actually describing the shape of the moral life. This book then is not so much a textbook in Christian virtue ethics as it is an argument for how the Christian life should actually be lived today.

In the next six chapters I will give an account of three virtues and three practices that guide faithful witness to the gospel. In one chapter I will describe a virtue, and in the following chapter

I will describe a practice that is formed by and forms that virtue. So the next chapter on the virtue of faith will be followed by a chapter on the practice of education. The chapter on hope will be followed by a chapter on worship, and the chapter on love will be followed by one on hospitality.

This pairing of virtues and practices draws on MacIntyre's argument that the virtues and practices are mutually corrective and sustaining.[35] Habituation in virtues appropriate to the gospel guides the formation of appropriate practices, and the appropriate practices further our habituation in the virtues. In all this we want to remember that our goal is faithfulness to the gospel.

In the chapters on the virtues I will consider faith, hope and love. In the theological tradition these virtues are "theological virtues" because we have them only by God's grace.[36] For my account, these virtues will be considered as they enable us to live according to the gospel.

In the chapters on the practices I will consider education, worship and hospitality. In the theological tradition these practices are not as clearly identified as the virtues. Nevertheless I will show how they and the virtues are necessary to sustaining our witness to the gospel.

Neither the virtues and practices nor our witness to the gospel occurs in a vacuum. All of these must be related to the particular situation in which the church lives. Therefore in the following chapters I will give considerable attention to our cultural situation because it is complex and controversial. Here I will briefly introduce the two terms, *modernity* and *postmodernity,* that I will use to characterize our situation.[37]

Modernity describes the culture that has shaped our recent history, at least since the seventeenth century. Reason, which is viewed as a universal possession of humanity, replaces religion as the guide to truth. Against the backdrop of the wars of religion that devastated Europe in the seventeenth and eighteenth centuries, reason is adopted as a means of securing peace. Humans are set free from the chains of superstition, religion and all other external authorities in order to establish themselves as individuals, governed only by autonomy, the authority of the individual. Nations and governments are formed as these autonomous individuals choose to associate with each other. Through reason humanity can conquer nature and use it to further its interests. In sum, the individual is at the center of the universe and can conquer everything through the powers that have been set free by the Enlightenment.

Postmodernity represents the passing of modernity. Postmodernity calls all the beliefs and practices of modernity into question. Reason is not some universal property of humanity but something that is constructed by different cultures in different ways. When these cultures confront each other, reason is as much a source of violence as is religion.[38] The individual (or, better, the *notion* of the individual) is also a construction of our culture. As a result, the individual does not really exist. Cultures, not individuals, are the real source of authority. Finally in the midst of an ever-deepening environmental crisis, postmodernity reveals that our supposed conquest of nature is, in the end, nature's conquest of humanity. In sum, humanity, in its attempt to conquer, merely reveals the "will to power" that perpetuates the ineradicable violence of the human condition.[39]

These two cultures mark the situation of the church in the West. As we will see, they represent dangers to and opportunities for faithful witness to the gospel. No matter what our cultural situation, the mission of the church is to live in faithfulness to the gospel as a witness to the world of God's salvation. The tragedy today is that all too often the virtues and practices embodied in the lives of Christians reveal conflicting beliefs about reality, even beliefs about reality that are contrary to the gospel. The reflections in this book are grounded in the hope that through learning from it and arguing with it the life of the church may more faithfully witness to the gospel of Jesus Christ by being conformed to him.

Three

FAITH AND THE
CHRISTIAN WAY
OF KNOWING

· · · · · · · · · · · · · · · · · · ·

W HAT CAN WE KNOW? HOW DO WE KNOW IT? HOW DO WE KNOW
that we know it? Can we be certain that we know what we claim
to know? When people claim to know something, are they merely
giving us their interpretation in order to preserve their power and
protect their interests? These are the questions that modernity
and postmodernity press upon us. Does the gospel of Jesus Christ
provide us with any guidance in this cultural situation? Or is it
about something called *faith*, not something called *knowledge?*

I will argue that the Christian virtue of faith guides the Christian
way of knowing and enables the church to witness faithfully to
the gospel in the midst of challenges to knowledge and truth in
our culture. Since any Christian account of virtues must be rooted
in the gospel and have as its aim more faithful witness to the
gospel, my primary purpose in this chapter is to give an account
of faith as a virtue formed by the gospel of Jesus Christ. But since
the aim of such an account is more faithful witness to the gospel
by a particular community located in a specific time and place,

I will also attend to these specific challenges presented by our cultural situation.

I will begin by considering faith in the Christian tradition. I will argue that we have wrongly neglected faith as a virtue and that by this neglect we are susceptible to the dangers of our cultural situation. My concern will not be to develop a full account of the virtue of faith but to consider what it means to think of faith as a virtue rather than as a purely mental or volitional act. I will also consider in some detail the characteristics of our cultural situation that represent dangers to the virtue of faith and opportunities for faithful witness to the gospel. Since this is my first detailed consideration of our cultural situation, this account will take some time to develop. Finally I will give an account of the virtue of faith as a guide to Christian knowing in the midst of modernity and postmodernity.

Faith in the Christian Tradition
Although faith has not been neglected in recent theology, most of us are not accustomed to thinking of faith *as a virtue*. As a result we have an emaciated understanding of faith that renders us vulnerable to the dangers of modernity and postmodernity. Even though it may be unfamiliar to us, thinking of faith as a virtue will help enliven our understanding of faith and enable us to be faithful.

We are susceptible to the dangers of modernity when we think of faith merely as a mental act of assent to a list of propositions, such as a statement of faith.[1] In this view humans may be reduced to disembodied minds who know "objective truth." But what we Christians know by faith is not just a list of propositions. What we know by faith is a person, Jesus Christ. Certainly the propositions are essential to identifying Jesus Christ, but they are not the object of our faith.

Moreover, we who know Jesus Christ by faith are not disembodied minds but persons. As persons we have our own history, our own personalities through which we come to faith. This does not lead to a vicious subjectivity but to an understanding of the virtue of faith as personal.

In addition to being susceptible to modernity, we may be susceptible to the dangers of postmodernity. This may happen when we think of faith as merely a volitional act of trust in Jesus Christ.[2] In this view, humans may be reduced to "the will to power." Faith, in this instance, is the destruction of my will by God's will. But when we know Jesus Christ by faith, our will is not defeated but transformed. Certainly the bondage of our will to sin is broken, but it is broken so that we may be set free to do the will of God.

As a virtue, faith is the means by which persons come to know the person of Jesus Christ and by which we are transformed in our knowing. Faith is not something that marks only one aspect of our humanity. It transforms our whole way of being and our whole way of living. Faith becomes the habit by which we live and know. Certainly there is a moment when we are "born again" to this new being and life in Christ. But just as we do not know the moment of our first birth, we do not necessarily know the moment of our rebirth by the power of the Spirit. And just as we grow and mature after our first birth, so also we grow and mature after our rebirth. Habituation in the virtue of faith is one sign of growth in this new life. By this habituation in faith we grow in knowledge and are better able to be faithful witnesses to the gospel in the midst of modernity and postmodernity.

Why We Need Faith as a Virtue

We live in a time when cultural transformation is taking place at the center of our lives, not just at its periphery. This transformation presents followers of Jesus Christ with dangers and temptations that threaten to corrupt faithful witness to the gospel, but it also presents opportunities for understanding the gospel more profoundly and witnessing to it more faithfully.

The pathos of knowledge. We have all encountered—and sometimes, perhaps often—adopted views of knowledge that are rooted in our cultural situation rather than in the gospel. Our culture's traditional understanding of knowledge has been formed by the assumptions of modernity. Now, however, that modern tradition is breaking down in a time that many characterize as postmodern.[3] Both the language of *breaking down* and *postmodern* emphasize that we are in a time of transition: *breaking down* describes a process, not a completed state of affairs, and *postmodern* merely tells us that we live in a time after the dominance of the culture of modernity. It is still unclear where we are going to end up as a culture, at least for any significant period of time. But even in this time of transition, perhaps especially in this time of transition, new understandings of knowledge have challenged our culture's tradition.

Two errors. Times of transition pose special dangers for those seeking to remain faithful to the gospel. In changing times, we can make two errors.

One is to elevate the previous culture to canonical status. We view the previous culture's understanding of truth and knowledge as something that we must defend against contemporary challenges—for the sake of the gospel. This temptation may be particularly appealing when we have worked out a series of responses to the previous culture's questions. So, for example, if evangelical Christianity has worked out evangelistic and apologetic strategies in relation to modernity (as I believe we have), then modernity is a more familiar and comfortable culture than is postmodernity. Attacks on that familiar culture may also appear to be attacks on evangelical Christianity. But such attacks are not in essence attacks on evangelical theology or the gospel. Neither evangelical theology nor the gospel is dependent on one particular culture, so we must not make the mistake of defending the previous culture in place of the gospel.

The second error is directly related to the success we have had in the previous culture: we may fall into the trap of simply repeating to a changing culture our responses to and strategies for faithfulness in the previous culture. In a new situation the challenges to our culture's traditional understanding of knowledge are also opportunities for a new articulation of the shape of faithful Christian living and witness.

Opportunities. Having lived with modernity for so long, theology and the church in European cultures have developed an understanding of the gospel in relation to those cultures—some accommodating the culture, some rejecting the culture, and many shades of response in between.[4] Now as modernity breaks down we have an opportunity to gain new insights into the gospel.[5] This has often occurred to societies that went through cultural change and to Christians who have moved from their home culture to another or encountered Christians from another culture.[6]

Our calling is to discern how to be faithful witnesses to the gospel through the guidance and enabling of the Holy Spirit in the midst of our world. In a postmodern age then our calling is not to denounce postmodernity but to witness to the gospel. Of course, that witness is itself a judgment of all our human creations, including postmodernity, but we must always remember that God's judgment has as its ultimate goal redemption, not destruction.

In relation to the virtue of faith, new insights into the gospel's way of knowing arise as we consider the breakdown of modernity and the rise of postmodernity. These new insights illuminate the ways in which we have accommodated modernity. They also provide us with potential responses to the pathos of postmodernity.

Knowledge in Modernity and Postmodernity

Where modernity is optimistic and confident about the possibilities of human knowing, postmodernity is pessimistic and skeptical. Against modernity's understanding of knowledge as objective and impersonal correspondence with reality, postmodernity argues that knowledge is an interpretation of reality or, more radically, a construction of reality. Against modernity's quest for certainty in knowledge, postmodernity stresses the uncertainty that attends all forms of knowledge. Against modernity's supposedly disinterested search for truth, postmodernity exposes the quest for power and the protection of power inherent in any claim to knowledge.

Since we live in a time of cultural change marked by the breaking down of modernity, we can best identify the pathos of knowledge in our culture and the challenges it presents by attending to the postmodernist understanding of knowledge. Two central postmodern views of knowledge prevail: knowledge as interpretation and knowledge as power.

Knowledge as interpretation. One of the most prolific and influential advocates for a postmodernist understanding of knowledge as interpretation is Richard Rorty. As represented by Rorty, postmodernity attacks the modernist view of knowledge as the correspondence between our mental notions and an external reality. In place of this Rorty argues that knowledge is interpretation.[7] He seeks to replace epistemology, the branch of philosophy that studies how we know what we know, with hermeneutics. He also seeks to replace an understanding of hermeneutics as the method by which we obtain truth with an understanding of hermeneutics as a practice by which we are edified.[8]

In their attack on modernist notions of truth postmodernists such as Rorty argue that the traditional quest for knowledge produces trivial or doubtful results.[9] Developing a call for an ongoing conversation, they argue that knowledge is simply one interpretation interacting with another interpretation interacting with another interpretation . . . *ad infinitum.*[10] This conversation among interpretations leads us not to truth but to other interpretations, which lead us to still other interpretations, again *ad infinitum*. The aim of this conversation is not truth but a more humane society.[11]

Something similar to this view marks our everyday lives whenever we operate with the conviction that "everyone is entitled to his or her own opinion." This conviction typically reflects the underlying judgments that we are dealing with an area where truth is either unobtainable or where it is more important to keep the peace than to challenge a statement. These two judgments reflect precisely Rorty's arguments that (1) truth is trivial and (2) the aim of philosophy is to keep the conversation going in order to form a more humane society. Another way of putting the latter would be to agree with Rorty that democracy is more important than philosophy—that getting along and letting each person have his or her say matters more than arriving at the truth.

Knowledge as power. Intertwined with this claim that knowledge is interpretation is a second challenge to the traditional understanding of knowledge. If knowledge is simply an interpretation of reality advanced by one person, tradition or community, then claims to knowledge, at bottom, mask or reveal a quest for power.[12] Of course, modernity also viewed knowledge as power, but this power was rooted in the conviction that knowledge was access to reality—that is, knowledge enabled us to do things with reality. Today the claim that "knowledge is power" reflects a very different conviction.

If knowledge is simply one interpretation or construction of reality among other competing interpretations or constructions of reality produced by a person, community or tradition, then knowledge is not access to reality. Instead, claims to knowledge merely represent access to, or attempts to access, power on behalf of a person, community or tradition. In this situation knowledge is anything that I can get others to accept as true or that gains power for me, my community or my tradition. This acceptance forms an "interpretive community" that then becomes a base for extending power.[13]

This struggle for power marks many of the debates in academia with which we are so familiar, such as those over the literary canon, over Columbus's discovery—or invasion—of America and over ethnic studies programs.[14] It also enters the public arena in debates about social issues and government policy. Today politics is marked not by a concern with truth but by a concern with what the public *perceives* to be true. As a result, our social policy debates are shaped by innumerable polls of public opinion that enable us to form bases of power.

Postmodern anxiety. Together these postmodern attacks on modernity's understanding of knowledge can cause us great anxiety. They reflect and abet the changes in our culture that cause such distress and turmoil in society. Political arguments no longer seem to be concerned with knowledge of the truth. Now they are simply a quest for power by my special group. Truth, it seems, can be twisted into anything that advances my interpretation of reality and my quest for power. Conflicts are resolved not by our mutual capitulation to "the truth" but only by the dominance or victory of one side or another.[15]

Deepening this distress is the loss of belief in knowledge as a path to certainty. Modernity's quest for knowledge was ultimately an optimistic quest for certainty about the world and humanity's place in the world. But if knowledge is an interpretation of how I propose, or my community proposes, to view reality, and if such claims to knowledge are an exercise of power, then we must also abandon as hopeless the traditional quest for knowledge that is certain. As a result, the postmodern age is marked by deep skepticism about the certainty of human knowledge. The best that we can hope for, it seems, is that those who gain power will create a more humane world.[16]

The distress in our culture exposed by these postmodernist arguments is even more intense for Christians than for society in general. For society, debates about the nature of knowledge are contests for political power and are also contests for one or another view of our society. But for Christians the meaning of these debates is even deeper. They are debates about people's relationship to God—or, better, about God's relationship to individuals—and about people's eternal destiny. Questions about knowledge are most acute.

The temptation of modernity. In this situation Christians are faced with three temptations that will lead them astray, away from faithful witness to the gospel. As I develop an account of Christian faith as a virtue, I will return to these temptations to demonstrate how wrong they are and how the virtue of faith exposes and corrects their errors. The first two temptations are fairly straightforward; the third is more subtle.

The first temptation lures us into support for modernity. Since Christianity in the West has lived with modernity for so long and since we have developed articulate responses to modernity, this temptation is strong. Faced with the uncertainty of postmodernity, we may long for the good old days when we knew the challenges to Christian faith and had well-developed responses to them.[17] Alternatively if we believe that the only way to talk about truth is in the language and categories of modernity, we will believe that the survival of witness to the truth of the gospel depends on the survival of modernity.

But as I will argue further in my account of the virtue of faith, the categories of modernity are not the only way to argue about truth or to witness to the gospel. Indeed, modernity has often exercised a corrupting influence on Christian witness to the gospel. The breaking down of modernity has enabled us to see some ways in which we Christians have misconstrued the truth of the gospel. For example, modernity views knowledge as a mental act by which we grasp an object or, more broadly, an objective reality. Christian faith, however, is not knowledge of an object or an objective reality in the modernist sense. Rather,

Christian faith, as we will see in more detail, is knowing and being known by a subject, a person—Jesus Christ.

Now we can also see how the forces of modernity may corrupt our understanding of faith as a mental act of assent. When we think of faith in this way we are seeking to establish faith as knowledge on the ground that modernity has established for what counts as knowledge. But to do so is to accommodate the culture and emaciate the gospel. How this is so will become clearer when I develop an account of the virtue of faith.[18]

The temptation of postmodernity. The second temptation lures us in two ways into wholehearted support for postmodernity. First, we support postmodernity because we see it as a way of reintroducing Christianity into Western intellectual life. If everyone's opinion is equally valid, then Christian convictions are as valid as anyone else's. What right, on postmodern grounds, has the academy or any other intellectual endeavor to exclude Christianity? This temptation may be felt most acutely by those who have been excluded from intellectual debate because their Christian convictions are, on modernist grounds, not objective or neutral.[19]

The second way in which postmodernity lures the support of Christians is in its turn from knowledge to feeling. In some parts of the church, people have concluded that modernity has effectively destroyed any claim to knowledge by faith and have turned faith into a matter of feeling rather than knowledge. Postmodernity seems tailor-made for Christian witness. The unprecedented quest for spiritual experience in our society is illustrated by bestsellers such as *The Celestine Prophecy* and *A Course in Miracles*. We may be tempted to package the gospel as an answer to this quest, but such a quest is an expression of "consumer spirituality" that turns the gospel into something that meets my needs as I perceive them, not a genuine "thirst for God" that participates in the redemption of the gospel. Certainly this postmodern spiritual quest may be an opportunity for witness to the gospel. But we must be sure that we are witnessing to the gospel that transforms our desires and habituates us in faith in Jesus Christ.[20]

Although postmodernity offers opportunities for a more faithful witness to the gospel, it also threatens to corrupt our witness. If we use postmodernity as a way of creating space in our culture for the claims of the gospel, we may be drawn into the vicious power struggles of the postmodern condition. We may simply view the gospel as another way of expressing the "will to power." If we use the ascendancy of "feeling" prevalent in some versions of postmodernity, we may reduce the gospel to another version of emotivism.[21] The gospel will simply become a way that we feel about various things. In the midst of these threats and opportunities, we need habituation in faith in Jesus Christ in order to be witnesses of the gospel.

In the midst of uncertain times we are greatly tempted simply to choose sides in the struggle between modernity and postmodernity. But to do so would be to miss an opportunity to discover once again the radical claims and challenge of the good news of Jesus Christ. If we reject the alternatives presented to us, we then face a third temptation. Considering this temptation will also reveal why I have not provided a more stringent critique of the understandings of knowledge represented by modernity and postmodernity.

The temptation of epistemology. The third temptation that we face lures us to accept the ground on which the debate is being engaged. I have already suggested that we should not choose sides, but now I am further suggesting that we should not accept the very way the debate is set up. At present the debate is about knowledge—more specifically about *how* we know what we know—not about *what* or *whom* we know. In philosophical terms the debate is about the success or failure of epistemology.

One of the hallmarks of modernity is the number of attempts to provide a theory that will unify our knowledge and guarantee the certainty of our knowledge. One of the hallmarks of post-modernity is the number of attacks on these quests for episte-mological certainty. But as I will argue in my account of the virtue of faith, to accept epistemology as the ground of the debate commits Christians to a misconstrual of the gospel.[22]

Now it is clear why I did not have available a simple and straightforward response to the temptations of modernity and postmodernity. Most of the debate, at this point, is set in terms of the status and claims of epistemology. The solution for Christians to get beyond the objectivism of modernity and the relativism threatened by postmodernity is not to begin with a quest for another—"new and improved"—epistemology.[23] Rather, we must turn once again to the gospel to discover the "Christian way of knowing" taught by faith.

The Virtue of Faith and the Christian Way of Knowing

If we are to meet the challenges of our cultural situation, we must have an understanding of the Christian way of knowing that is guided by the gospel. This way of knowing comes only as we are habituated in the virtue of faith. Four aspects of faith in the New Testament will guide our account of the relationship between the virtue of faith and the Christian way of knowing: New Testament faith is personal; it is a gift; it is communal; and it is cosmic in scope.[24]

Faith as personal. In Jesus Christ we are given the ground and goal of faith. Since Jesus Christ is a person, Christian faith is faith in a person.[25] It is not faith in humanity, ideas or concepts. When we say that New Testament faith is faith in a person, Jesus Christ, we utter an obvious and commonplace assertion that conceals some profound implications, for the very form of the Gospels serves to identify Jesus as a person.[26] The Gospels are not compilations of "the sayings of Jesus Christ" or his ideas, they are witnesses to the identity of the person of Jesus and the redemp-tion accomplished through him. Likewise, the Acts of the Apostles and the other writings of the New Testament seek to continue the identification of the person of Jesus Christ through his work as the resurrected one. So we are being faithful to the New Testament when we assert that, for the Christian, faith is faith in a person.

If we through faith are to know Jesus Christ as a person, then the virtue of faith must be personal. It is personal not in the sense of "private" but in the sense that it involves our whole being. What we know or, better, who we know by faith is a person. Further, how we know him involves our whole person. Faith, in this sense, transforms us as persons. It is not merely the transformation of what we know or how we know, nor is it merely an act of the will. Rather, faith is the transformation of everything we are as persons. It is the creation of a new being in Jesus Christ by the power of the Holy Spirit.

This new being is characterized by the habits of faith that mark a new way of life, which is reoriented in every way to Jesus Christ. Thus for those who are being habituated by faith in Jesus Christ, all that we truly know and all that we long to know is revealed in him. We may be tempted then to think of faith as something that only pertains to a restricted sphere of our lives, but our knowing Jesus Christ by faith governs all of our knowing.

Since the virtue of faith transforms our entire being, we should not think of it as restricted to one area of who we are as humans. Faith is not merely mental assent or volitional consent, it is the habituation of the whole person in life with Jesus Christ so that our very way of assenting and consenting is also transformed. How this is so will become clearer as we consider how the virtue of faith guides the Christian way of knowing.

Knowing as personal. To say that the virtue of faith is personal is to say that our knowing cannot be reduced to a mental act.[27] We do not know other persons as persons by turning them into concepts or ideas, nor do we know them as persons through a purely mental act of our own. Rather, we know them through their whole way of life as persons, through our whole being as persons.

Against modernity, saying that faith is personal teaches us that our knowing cannot be reduced to a detached, objective stance. Persons are known, as Martin Buber famously reminded us, through I-Thou, not I-It, relationships.[28] This does not lead to a vicious subjectivity but to a relationship of subject to subject. If we are to remain faithful to the gospel, we must not reduce our knowledge of Christ to a subject-object relationship or, in the worst manifestations of modernity, an object-object relationship, where an impersonal mind knows an impersonal concept. Rather, our knowing Christ, which comes as we are habituated in faith, is a subject-subject relationship. This way of knowing depends not on an objective, detached, neutral stance but on the passionate commitment of our whole being.

Therefore over against the modernist notion that knowledge is objective, the virtue of faith teaches that our knowing is personal. This way of knowing does not condemn us to subjectivity but frees us to know all things through the person of Christ. Against the postmodernist claim that since objective knowledge is not possible therefore knowledge is not possible, the virtue of faith teaches that all true knowing is found through the person of Jesus Christ. As Lesslie Newbigin argues, "The great objective reality is God but he is also the supreme subject who wills to make himself known to us not by a power that would cancel out our subjectivity, but by a grace that calls forth and empowers our subjective faculties, our power to grow in knowledge through believing."[29]

Faith as a gift. In the New Testament, faith in the person of Jesus Christ comes not through human initiative or achievement but by God's gift. Since faith is knowing the person of Jesus Christ, it begins with God's initiative in the sending of God's Son. It continues as we who are dead in our trespasses and sins are made alive in Christ by the power of the Holy Spirit.

At this point the gospel exercises a profound change in the traditional understanding of virtue. In most virtue ethics, virtue is an achievement of human effort, but in the gospel, virtue comes as a gift. Faith understood in this way does not fit the language of virtue. Faith seems to be something alien to us, not something that marks our being. Precisely here we must recall that *Christian* ethics does not seek to describe better lives, it seeks to describe new lives in Christ. And one character trait, one virtue, that marks new life in Christ is faith. It is not our old lives that display the virtue of faith, it is our new lives.

New life is given by God, not achieved by persons, but it is given by God so that we may become new persons. In relation to life apart from Christ, faith is a gift. In relation to new life in Christ, this gift is a virtue.[30] So for Christians, faith is a virtue rooted in God's gift.

This understanding of the virtue of faith as a gift reminds us that, for followers of Jesus Christ, the virtues must be transformed by the gospel. In this instance our lives are transformed by the gospel, and faith is one of the virtues that marks transformed lives.

Knowing as a gift. This conception of faith as a gift teaches much about the Christian way of knowing. For those who are new persons in Christ, all knowing is a gift. There may be other kinds of knowing, but *for Christians* all knowing is a gift. This means, of course, that what people know is received, not achieved. Furthermore, it teaches that all truly Christian knowing is the result of humility, not pride, and therefore should lead to humility, not pride. Humility, not enlightenment, is the first step toward the Christian way of knowing.

This account of Christian knowing runs directly counter to modernist conceptions of how we achieve knowledge. According to modernity knowledge is achieved through human effort, not received as a divine gift. The quest for knowledge is a quest to master the world, not a submission to being mastered by God's gift in Jesus Christ. The ability to receive this gift from God requires and shapes virtues very different from those called for by a modernist conception of knowledge.[31] Only by God's grace may we be humble recipients of that gift that shapes our way of knowing.[32]

This account of Christian knowing also equips us to respond to postmodernist skepticism about human knowledge. If all we have is a modernist conception of knowledge, then when "faith" in that conception of knowledge begins to break down we are left with the conclusion that we cannot know. Postmodern claims to knowledge are simply disguised bids for power. Christians, formed by the virtue of faith, respond to this situation in three ways.

First, they offer an alternative conception of the path to knowing—knowing as a gift, not an achievement. The breaking down of modernity is false comfort if the only alternative is the pathos of postmodernity. Christians must be ready and able to present the claims of Jesus Christ as good news.

Second, Christians reject the claim that knowledge is mere interpretation. The Christian way of knowing and the knowledge that comes by way of that knowing are given by God in the gospel of Jesus Christ. Yes, Christians are called to the task of interpretation, but that task is supremely the task of interpreting the world according to the gospel of Jesus Christ, not interpreting the gospel to fit the demands of the world. In other words, the gospel, by the power of the Holy Spirit, teaches, reminds, convicts and guides (Jn 14-16).

Third, Christians refuse to enter the contest for power. Gifts cannot be forced on anyone, they can only be offered. These are difficult disciplines to practice, but they are necessary expressions of the peaceableness that marks those who know that their lives and all their knowing has been given to them.

Thus the virtue of faith as a gift shapes new lives. It calls us to be humble and receptive. It equips us to resist nostalgia for modernity and to witness faithfully to the gospel in a postmodern age.

Faith as communal. This gift of faith comes to us from God through a community, namely, the disciple community.[33] Before I develop this claim, I must identify three potential misunderstandings of what I mean by *communal*.[34]

First, by *communal* I do not mean to place my account within the context of the communitarian movement often identified with Amitai Etzioni and William Bennett. This movement seeks to rebuild communities in order to shore up or restore American democracy. That purpose and the communities and virtues for which it calls are very different from the purpose of the disciple community and the virtues of the gospel.[35]

Second, by *communal* I do not mean that faith is solely for the sake of a particular community, the church. The church's mission is beyond the church—it is to witness to the world of God's redemption.

Third, by *communal* I do not refer to a community like any other. In the tradition of virtue ethics, virtues are formed by a particular community with a particular conception of the *telos*. So to say that the community of faith is unlike any other community is a profound claim. Certainly the church is a human community, an "earthen vessel."[36] But it is also more than a human community—it is the body of Christ, a new community, the community of the redeemed.[37] The *telos* or, better, the eschaton that guides this community is not created by human beings, nor is it achieved by human effort. Rather, as we will see in the next chapter, the eschaton that guides the Christian community is the work of God that redeems creation.

To say that faith is communal reminds us that faith comes only through the witness of the disciple community. The mission of this community is to preach the gospel with its whole life so that others may believe. Even when someone comes to faith in circumstances seemingly far removed from the church, that conversion may be ultimately traced to the church.[38]

Consider someone with no previous exposure to the gospel who opens a Bible and reads it in a language which the Holy Spirit uses to bring that person to faith. Even in this seemingly remote instance, the existence of that Bible is due to a faithfully witnessing church. So to say that faith is communal is to say that we come to faith only through the existence of a community that continues to witness to the work of God in Jesus Christ.

But to say that faith is communal is to say more—it is to say that faith is formed and sustained only in the community of Jesus Christ. Here we draw on one of the central insights of virtue ethics: virtue is not something to be added to an account of individual morality in order to round it off. Virtue reconceives the realm of morality, denying among other things the distinction between individual and social ethics. People become persons only in and through a particular community. Therefore which community shapes us as persons is a matter of inestimable import.

From the Christian viewpoint, the community that teaches the virtue of faith is the church. This claim has many implications, two of which are significant here. First, only in the disciple community do we find the gifts of the Spirit which are necessary to the formation of faith.[39] In this community the diverse gifts of the Spirit complement each other and correct the tendency of Christians to drift away from faith. Second, in this community the diverse gifts of the Spirit keep our knowledge of the gospel alive, enabling us to discern the work of the gospel today, participate in that work and be formed by our participation in it.[40]

Knowing as communal. These implications of the claim that faith is communal guide the Christian way of knowing. In the disciple community this claim corrects our tendency to concentrate responsibility for knowing in one area of giftedness or in one office of the community. Certainly the church needs intellectuals, theologians, people who are teachers. But the disciple community also needs other gifted people: administrators, who insure that everyone's voice is heard; the merciful, who attach ideas to people; prophets, who are sensitive to new direction from the Spirit of God; and so on. Only when this diversity of gifts is honored does the church embody the Christian way of knowing.[41]

When the church practices the virtue of faith as communal, it is also equipped to meet the challenges of today. Against the tendency of modernity to view knowing as a solitary, individualistic achievement, the virtue of faith teaches that Christian knowing is the practice of a gifted community.[42] This deepens the significance of humility as the first step in Christian knowing and teaches the indispensability of charity toward others and engenders a profound practice of friendship.

Although this call to the virtue of faith as communal reflects a Christian transformation of one aspect of postmodernity—namely, the claim by many postmodernists that our knowing is inescapably communal—it corrects two other tendencies of postmodernity that threaten faithfulness to the gospel. First, against the postmodernist tendency to view communities in terms of an interminable power struggle, it reminds us that our communal knowing is a gift to be shared, not a power to be imposed. Second, against the fear that postmodernity leads to a vicious relativism, the practice of faith as communal affirms that knowing is relative to a particular *telos,* Jesus Christ. But that way of knowing is not a vicious relativism, it is simply a restatement of the conviction that "in [Christ] are hidden all the treasures of wisdom and knowledge" (Col 2:3).

Against the fear that postmodernity leads to subjectivity, the practice of faith as communal forces us to rely on the Spirit-gifted community, not on ourselves as individuals. The accusation of subjectivity makes sense only if knowing is an individual achievement or if the community neglects or suppresses the work of the Spirit. It does not make sense if we practice knowing as a communal gift truly under the guidance of the Spirit.[43]

The virtue of faith as communal teaches that Christian faith is formed in us only through the Spirit-gifted community. Through the life and practices of this community, we come to know Jesus Christ as our errors and sins are identified, judged and forgiven. Through the gifts of the Spirit in this community, our knowing is properly guided and we are equipped to meet the challenges of our cultural situation. The threats of modernity and postmodernity are not only disarmed, they are also met with an alternative way of knowing that witnesses to the redemption of creation in Jesus Christ.

Faith as cosmic. Since the community that forms faith witnesses to and serves an end (an eschaton) that promises the redemption of creation, the virtue of faith changes our stance toward the entire creation. This assertion has its roots in Paul's cosmic Christology, most clearly expressed in his letter to the Colossians:

> [Christ] is the image of the invisible God, the first born of all creation; for in him all things in heaven and on earth were created, things visible and invisible, whether thrones or dominions or rulers or powers—all things have been created through him and for him. He himself is before all things, and in him all things hold together. (1:15-17)
>
> In [Christ] are hidden all the treasures of wisdom and knowledge. (2:3)

The cosmic claims of these passages may tempt us to soften their impact and narrow their scope, but understanding faith as a virtue that guides the Christian way of knowing helps us accept and practice their full force. When we confront these passages, we may think that Paul surely does not mean that we can know such things as geography, psychology and calculus through Christ. But if we consider faith as a virtue, we can see how Paul claims precisely that. Only through Christ do we know things in their proper relationship and in reality.

In another portion of the Colossian passage Paul asserts that "through [Christ] God was pleased to reconcile to himself all things" (1:20). This is the reality of all things in heaven and on earth: they need reconciliation to God, and that reconciliation has been accomplished through Jesus Christ. We may "know" all sorts of things, but we do not know them truly until we know this momentous truth: through Christ God has reconciled them to himself. This knowledge comes only as we know ourselves to be reconciled to Christ. When we know the person of Christ through the gift of faith in the community of the Spirit, then and only then can we begin to know all things.

So the virtue of faith is cosmic. Since faith is a virtue that transforms the being of a person, then all that person comes to know is shaped by that virtue. But we may still wonder if all that we know is really characterized by faith. Through Paul's claims about Jesus Christ, we can now see that all knowing is to be found through him. The Christian way of knowing is cosmic.

Knowing as cosmic. This means that all the ways in which we know must be transformed by the virtue of faith. However we may construe what it means to be human, there is no area of our humanity untouched by the claims of faith. How we know—through our emotions, our wills, our minds, our bodies—must be shaped by the virtue of faith in order to conform to the Christian way of knowing. The claim that faith is cosmic also means that everything we know must be shaped by the virtue of faith. No area of human knowledge escapes the claims of faith as a virtue. The virtue of faith as cosmic equips us to meet and correct a number of challenges in our cultural situation.

Against the secularization of modernity that isolates faith in one particular sphere and denies it the status of knowledge, the virtue of faith as cosmic teaches us that we only know those "other" things if we know them by faith. Where modernity alienates the knower from the known and then struggles vainly to overcome that alienation through epistemology, faith declares that all things have been reconciled in Christ and that through that reconciliation we can know all things in their proper relationship to God.

Against the postmodernist capitulation to alienation and its abandonment of epistemology in favor of the will to power, the virtue of faith as cosmic again witnesses to the reconciliation of all things in and through Christ. Against the postmodernist rejection of any metanarrative—that is, any account of the cosmos—the virtue of faith teaches that the gospel is a metanarrative of reconciliation, not an ill-disguised bid for power.[44]

The virtue of faith as cosmic then teaches us that all our knowing comes by faith in Jesus Christ. This corrects the tendency of the church both to restrict faith to a special sphere and status and to grant the status of knowledge to things known apart from the gospel of Jesus Christ. The virtue of faith as cosmic calls the disciple community to a more profound and disciplined practice that will faithfully witness to a world marked by skepticism and alienation.

Conclusion

Is faith a virtue? If we take seriously the account of faith that I have just given, then it makes sense to think of faith as a virtue. Certainly faith is planted in us by new birth in the Spirit, but as we grow in new life that faith develops and matures. As we cooperate with the Spirit, we are habituated in faith.

Moreover, faith in Jesus Christ is not a mark of only one aspect of our humanity, it transforms our entire being. In Jesus Christ faith comes to us as a gift, but that gift is the mark of our new life in Christ and we grow in that new life. Furthermore, our growth in faith depends on our participation in the disciple community. We participate in many different communities in our lives, but if the disciple community is not determinative for our lives, then our faith is emaciated or even stillborn. In Jesus Christ faith is given its goal, its *telos* in the eschaton.

In this chapter I have used the concepts of virtue ethics, as transformed by the gospel, to give an account of the virtue of faith that is rooted in the gospel of Jesus Christ. This account is itself an argument for the recovery of faith as a virtue that forms the Christian way of knowing. Such a recovery would enable us who compose the church to witness faithfully to the gospel in our present situation by confessing our faith before the questions of modernity and postmodernity.

To the question "What can we know?" Christians who are habituated in faith answer, "It's not *what* you know, it's *who* you know." And we ask in response, "Do you know Jesus Christ?"[45]

To the question "How do we know?" Christians respond, "By the gift of faith in Jesus Christ." And we ask in return, "Do you have that faith?"

To the question "How can we be certain of what we know?" faith teaches us to respond, "Certainty is not grounded in human powers but in God's gift and the gifts of the disciple community." And we ask, "Are you a member of that community?"

To the postmodern suspicion that all knowing is an exercise in power, we offer faith as a gift that transforms our will to power and teaches us to live peaceably. For too long the disciple community has accepted the modernist construal of knowledge that denies to faith the status of knowledge. Postmodernity has helped expose the errors of modernity, but only the gospel can provide us with a sure guide for our knowing. Far from being something other than knowledge, faith is the only way by which we can know all things truly—as reconciled to God in and through Jesus Christ.

In this chapter I have commended the virtue of faith as the Christian way of knowing. However, I have not yet described how the virtue of faith may be recovered and formed in us. For that we must look to the practices of the church that inculcate faith. So we continue our consideration of the virtue of faith in the next chapter.

Four

FORMING FAITH

Education as a Practice

. . . .

W̲E HAVE EXPLORED THE CHRISTIAN VIRTUE OF FAITH IN RELA-tion to the tradition of the church and the pathos of knowledge in our culture. The virtue of faith habituates us into a relationship to Jesus Christ that changes our way of knowing and enables us to be faithful witnesses to the gospel in a world where knowledge has failed. For us, the church as the "disciple community," to be habituated in the virtue of faith that shapes our way of knowing, we must attend to the way in which faith forms us and is formed in us through the practice of education.

Imagine a family named Neal. The daughter, Laura, has just been admitted to five colleges and universities, and the Neal family is sitting down to talk about which school Laura should attend. If they are Christians, what criteria will they apply? Should Laura attend a college that provides her with social connections that will almost certainly guarantee her a successful career in the corridors of power? Should she attend a university that has the most prestigious faculty and the smartest students? Should she attend a Christian college? What would a "Christian education" look like?[1]

In this chapter I will describe education as a practice that forms and is formed by the virtue of faith. First, I will identify what I mean by the *practice* of education. In this account *practice* has a particular meaning that illuminates a number of issues. Second, I will examine one popular way of talking about moral education in relation to the virtues—namely, "character development"—and show why that language fails as a description of the practice of education that forms faith. This examination exposes some further issues that I address in the final section as I develop an account of the practice of education. Before turning to those accounts, however, I must identify one potential misunderstanding that could lead us astray.

When we think of education, we often think of a formal classroom setting, perhaps in a school, a church or even a business. The classroom is set apart from other areas of life for the purpose of education. Although the example of the Neal family selecting a college plays into this understanding, I will be considering education in much broader terms. I will seek to describe a faithful practice of education that we are involved in throughout our lives, in all areas of our lives.[2]

If the virtue of faith transforms our entire being and engages our whole life, then every activity either forms or deforms the virtue of faith. So although the practice of education described here may seem strange, it seems that way only because we have drifted so far from education as a practice rooted in the gospel.

Thomas Howard's autobiography *Christ the Tiger* exemplifies this understanding of education.[3] The book is really the story of Howard's education in faith. Some of his education takes place in various classrooms, but most of it takes place in settings such as family devotions, the family business, church, army barracks, social occasions and walks with friends. Howard learns in all these different settings, and he is shaped in his whole person.

Howard's story will provide us with various insights as we consider the practice of education.[4]

Education as a Practice

Practices may be engaged in by a variety of communities and may reflect various understandings of the virtues. In all this variety, practices exhibit five characteristics that MacIntyre identifies.[5] But it would be a mistake simply to give an account here of these five characteristics apart from their particular shape within the living tradition of the gospel. What concerns us is the practice of education that is shaped by, and in turn shapes, the "gospel virtue" of faith.[6] So as we consider the five characteristics of a practice, I will have in view education as a practice of the church that forms faith rooted in the gospel.

First, for education to be a "practice" it must be a complex activity. This complexity will be evident throughout my account, especially in the way the forming of faith involves God's grace and human transformation.[7]

Second, education must be socially embodied. Christians find this social embodiment in the church as the community of disciples.

Third, education must realize goods "internal" to it. In other words, education must not be for something beyond the practice of education, such as fame, success or fortune. Rather, what education accomplishes as a practice must be internal to the practice of education. This is a complex claim that will become clearer as I consider the practice of education that is proper for the gospel. Later in the chapter I will take the beatitudes of Jesus as an example of the practice of education that forms faith. There I will show that the "blessedness" of the beatitudes is internal to Jesus' practice of education.

Fourth, education must be rooted in a conception of the *telos*. For Christians, education is rooted in convictions about the eschaton, which is the coming of redemption in Jesus Christ.

Finally, education must extend our ability to participate in the virtues and in the eschaton that identifies our community. All of these characteristics will guide my account of the practice of education and will be exemplified in that account.[8]

To describe education as a practice is not the same as describing an educational theory, nor is *practice* another word for *method*. The quest for a theory and a method is a quintessentially modernist quest. Modernity teaches that since we are fundamentally alienated as knowers, the quest for a theory (of knowledge, for example) seeks to provide a justification for how we come to know. Method then becomes the means by which we apply the theory. Although they seem much the same thing, the differences between practice and method are especially significant.

On the one hand, method belongs to the realm of *technical* reason. It denies our particularities as persons and considers us all capable of achieving knowledge if we will simply learn the proper method. Method views everything is an object to be manipulated. On the other hand, practice belongs to the realm of *practical* reason. It acknowledges the complexities of our particularities as persons and recognizes that no one approach fits everyone. Moreover, modernity's method may supposedly be applied without any real change in its practitioners. A practice, however, requires our participation and changes us through that participation.

Consider the importance of this distinction for forming faith through the practice of education. We do not all hear things and respond to them in the same way.[9] We must discern how our particularities—for example, temperament, age, status, race and sex—and the particularities of others shape the ways in which we respond to each other. What sounds like harsh criticism to one student is gentle admonishment to another.

Much education today seems quite amenable to the notion of method, but that is due to our capitulation to modernity. If education is to form faith in us, then we must resist the lure of method and seek instead a more complex and, for those shaped by modernity, an initially less satisfying *practice* of education.

If you are looking for a *method* by which to teach virtue, this chapter will be a disappointment. If, however, you are willing to enter into a practice that itself embodies the virtue of faith and habituates you in faith, this chapter will offer an account of the practice of education that seeks to be faithful to the virtue of faith.

Why Character Development Is Not Enough
In the current revival of virtue and character, some educators are giving more attention to the role of character development in education.[10] This attention may be helpful—similar to the way that I have viewed the rise of virtue ethics as helpful. But it also presents some dangers. We must not mistake it as an adequate description of the faithful practice of education.[11] The term *character development* itself presents two dangers, but a third danger lies in the way we relate the concept to conventional education.

The term *character* is itself problematic because it does not contain its own definition or description. As I argued above, virtue and character are shaped by a community and communal convictions about "the good life." When we use the term *character* in our discussions of education, we seldom examine precisely what we mean by it. If we do examine its meaning, we seldom if ever penetrate to an examination of the kind of community and conception of the *telos* that underlies our account of character.

Modernity treats the development of character as a matter for the individual to decide. We tell students that they should develop character, but we seldom tell them what kind of character they should develop. If we do give more specific guidance, we do not direct their character toward the gospel or the disciple community. As a result, we never identify the roots of the problems we are trying to correct through character development. The problem is not ultimately our need for character but our need for a particular kind of character, particular virtues rooted in the gospel and shaped by the disciple community. If we as Christians take seriously the virtues, community and eschaton revealed by the gospel of Jesus Christ, then we will often find ourselves in opposition to the assumptions about character development that we encounter in our society.

The root of our problems and the nature of our opposition may be identified as we consider the problems with the term *development*. Our adoption of that term assumes that we have within us the capacity for goodness that only needs to be developed. We are autonomous moral agents whose ability to act morally simply needs to be encouraged. But that is not what the gospel teaches.

The gospel reveals us to be incapable of true goodness apart from Christ. Our autonomy is not the source of morality but of immorality. Our capacity for goodness is not achieved through development but through the gift of new life in Christ. Put simply, "the Christian moral life is finally not one of development but of conversion."[12]

Last, a problem attends the notion of character development when it is simply added to conventional education as another element. This occurs when we think that education has several dimensions, one of which is character development. For example, some may think of education as a three-fold task: the transference of information, the production of knowledge and the formation of character. But this obscures the ways in which character is implicitly formed by how we transfer information and how we produce knowledge.

As Mark Schwehn has shown, the modernist approach to these matters forms virtues that are at odds with the gospel: "clarity, but not charity, honesty, but not friendliness, loyalty to calling, but not loyalty to particular, local communities."[13] Moreover, thinking of education as the transference of knowledge tends to treat teachers and students not as persons but as disembodied minds, as containers of knowledge. Thus if we simply add character development to other educational practices, we end up with an incoherent education whose elements are in conflict.

At this point I can now develop my reasons for retaining the term *education* rather than adopting some other word, such as *formation*. Although *formation* may seem to represent well the inculcation of virtues, I do not use the term because it is so often used to represent something that is added to other facets of education. I am not arguing that we need to add virtue to our educational practices, I am arguing that the gospel virtue of faith reconceives what we are doing in our practice of education. Therefore I take the risk of retaining the term *education* while at the same time seeking to subvert our usual understanding of that term. What we need is an account of the practice of education that forms in us the virtue of faith as revealed in the gospel.

The Practice of Education
In the previous chapter I identified four characteristics of the virtue of faith. Here we will consider those characteristics in reverse order as I seek to describe a practice of education that is formed by, and further forms, the virtue of faith. Again, what I am after is not a method but a practice—something more elusive and complex than a method. As I consider the first three characteristics of faith, I will turn for guidance to the book of Proverbs, a wonderful exemplar of the practice of education.[14]

Education as cosmic. To be a faithful practice, education must be cosmic. First, our practice of education must be cosmic in its concern for all knowing. We cannot restrict education to some special area of learning. When we attempt to narrow the concern of education, we distort the nature of what we know, we distort the humanity of teacher and learner and we thus distort our character. The book of Proverbs opens with a nice reminder of this:

The proverbs of Solomon son of David, king of Israel:
For learning about wisdom and instruction,
    for understanding words of insight,
for gaining instruction in wise dealing,
    righteousness, justice, and equity;
to teach shrewdness to the simple,
    knowledge and prudence to the young—
Let the wise also hear and gain in learning,
    and the discerning acquire skill,
to understand a proverb and a figure,
    the words of the wise and their riddles. (1:1-6)

In this passage various Hebrew words break up "the plain daylight of wisdom *(hokma)* into its rainbow of constituent colours."[15] These terms cover a whole range of knowing, from correction and reproof, through understanding and insight, wise-dealing and righteousness, to shrewdness and prudence.[16] The scope of these terms reminds us that education must be concerned with all our knowing, not restricted to one area. Our practice of education cannot ignore the need to give students information or to make them shrewd. But at the same time our practice of education cannot be content to give students information or teach them how to get along in the world or be successful without also attending to the way that their character is formed by such knowledge and skills.

In *Christ the Tiger* Thomas Howard continually exposes the interplay of knowledge and character as he is educated. In particular he struggles with the cosmic scope of faith as knowing. For a long time he seems to believe that he must choose between God and life, between the sacred and the secular. Along the way, however, Howard makes a friend, whom, he says,

worried me because he loved God and life at the same time. It had always been one or the other for me. When I had tried to pursue God, I had fled from life. When life began to be dazzling, I had let God slip. I would have called his voluptuous zest for life pagan, except that it was not only matched by his appetite for God: it was part of it. . . . I was jarred to discover that my friend had no dichotomy in his mind between spiritual things and other things. One was to love the world and experience because God did and because one loved God.[17]

The education provided by this friend and others eventually puts Howard on the path to the wisdom that views all of life as under God's rule.

Second, in the book of Proverbs the cosmic scope of our practice of education is concerned with what we do with what we know. Our practice of education must recognize the world's profound need for highly educated, highly skilled followers of Jesus Christ, but at the same time we must be aware of the profound dangers inherent in such knowing. In the structure of Proverbs we see just such a recognition.

Before commencing the series of proverbs in chapters 10-31 that will teach the student knowledge and skills for success, the author begins in chapters 1-9 with a series of "sermons" that prepare the student for wise use of all that he or she will learn. This preparation is accomplished by forming the community of faith within which wisdom is habituated and by directing that wisdom toward its proper *telos,* "the fear of the LORD" (1:7).[18] Likewise, our practice of education must continually remind us of the dangers inherent in our knowing and prepare us to know wisely by situating us within the disciple community and directing us toward the eschaton.

In our cultural situation the practice of education as cosmic confronts the contemporary rebellion of the world that goes by the name of *secularism.*[19] Secularism divides the world and confines God and faith to an increasingly smaller sphere. It is the conviction that there is something called the secular that is "out there," outside the control of any god that may exist.

This realm of the secular functions autonomously and must be studied by various expressions of human rationality, such as sociology, economics, psychology. Thus secularism creates "fields" or "disciplines" which we study and in which we live without reference to Christian convictions. Of course, many whose teaching is shaped by Christian convictions are in these disciplines. But when Christians teach political theory, anthropology, literature or religious studies *just like* it is taught at State U. or Private College, they succumb to secularism.

In ordinary life secularism creates spheres or areas of our lives that we wall off from God. When we divide life up into the sacred and the secular, we announce an intention to confine God and discipleship to Jesus Christ to the sacred. After making that distinction, we go on to reinforce the distinction through education.[20] For example, we may think that we can ignore theological questions in a course on economics as long as we add a course in business ethics to the curriculum. Or we may model for our children one rule in the home and another in social situations. But if our practice of education is to form faith, we must identify and overcome these kinds of dichotomies.

In our practice of education as cosmic, we ultimately must deny the existence of that realm that is called secular. The secular of secularism is not something given, it is not something discovered by humanity which we must simply accept. The secular is a creation of humanity. It is a rebellion against God, an attempt to drive God out of our world by constructing a world in which God does not exist and in which humans reign supreme. Having invented the secular, our culture has been busy increasing its sphere so that there is no room for a God who actually makes a difference in our lives.

Much education today forms us into this secularism by teaching that some things are sacred and other things are secular and by teaching us how to observe the proper boundaries. Even the educational practices of the church often—perhaps usually—reinforce this secularism by confining its educational aims to those areas of life marked off as sacred by our culture.

Recently a reporter from our local newspaper met with me to talk about the "religious" dimensions of the various stories that she covers. She began the conversation by telling me that many of her colleagues questioned the validity of covering the impact of Christian faith on education, business and politics. They argued that the paper had a Saturday "church page" and that religion should be confined to that kind of coverage. They did not want to let religion "get out of hand," and they were deeply suspicious of her motives for wanting to know more about religion.

In our society we often accept these kinds of restrictions and teach Christians to be nice, tolerant people fit for a democracy. Belief in God and following Jesus are acceptable as long as we observe the boundaries that have been set out and do not let our faith intrude on the secular.

The Christian name for the secular—a world where God is not present and humans have their way—is hell. Since our faith is cosmic and recognizes no boundaries around God's action in the universe, our practice of education must form students whose faith is cosmic, who acknowledge no boundaries to the knowing that is given by God in Christ.

Education as communal. For our practice of education to be faithful, it must be not only cosmic but also communal. Although the precise setting of the book of Proverbs is debated, it is clearly set within the context of the faithful community. In fact, it is the faith of the community that allows the sages to draw wisdom from a variety of sources, because they know that God is the source of all wisdom.[21] The responsibility of the community is to examine all claims to knowledge and convert them to faithfulness. Only in the disciple community do we find the diverse resources for discernment in this process of taking "every thought captive to obey Christ" (2 Cor 10:5).

As the community fulfills this responsibility, it has a further task: to teach through the practice of education how to relate all knowing to faith. In Proverbs we see a community at work teaching students how that community incorporates all knowing into its living tradition and directs all knowing toward its conception of "the good life." This is intellectual work at its most profound, difficult and rewarding. In our own society we may reflect this kind of community and its work in the acknowledgments section of a book such as this one. We should take very seriously the community represented by the naming of people who have contributed to our education.

Proverbs gives another example of the practice of education as communal. At least in part, the setting of Proverbs is the home, where father and mother practice the education that forms faith.[22] This practice reflects the instructions given in Deuteronomy:

> Now this is the commandment—the statutes and the ordinances—that the LORD your God charged me to teach you to observe in the land that you are about to cross into and occupy, so that you and your children and your children's children, may fear the LORD your God all the days of your life, and keep all his decrees and his commandments that I am commanding you, so that your days may be long. . . . Hear, O Israel: the LORD is our God, the LORD alone. You shall love the LORD your God with all your heart, and with all your soul, and with all your might. Keep these words that I am commanding you today in your heart. Recite them to your children and talk about them when you are at home and when you are away, when you lie down and when you rise. Bind them as a sign on your hand, fix them as an emblem on your forehead, and write them on the doorposts of your house and on your gates. (Deut 6:1-2, 4-9)

In this passage the cosmic and communal dimensions of the practice of education are combined. Education is to take place in the home: conversation at the dinner table is a place of education. Education is to take place in the world: shopping at the mall is an occasion for education. We must be continually, everywhere and always, conscious of ourselves as members of the community of disciples—we never leave that community behind.

In our practice of education we must always be aware that students are being formed into one community or another. Our practice of education should not make them "autonomous moral agents" but faithful members of the community of disciples. That community, not a person's academic discipline, profession or class, is determinative for our practice of education.

Education as a gift. Third, to be faithful, our practice of education must teach that knowing is a gift. It must embody humility and receptiveness. We may be tempted to think that this characteristic of faith and of the practice of education precludes effort and discipline on our part, but again the wisdom of Proverbs gives guidance:

> My child, if you accept my words
>   and treasure up my commandments within you,
> making your ear attentive to wisdom
>   and inclining your heart to understanding;
> if you indeed cry out for insight,
>   and raise your voice for understanding;
> if you seek it like silver,
>   and search for it as for hidden treasures—
> then you will understand the fear of the LORD
>   and find the knowledge of God.
> For the LORD gives wisdom;
>   from his mouth come knowledge and understanding.
> (2:1-6)

Here profound effort and discipline on the student's part result in the *gift* of wisdom and knowledge. Our practice of education must reflect this mystery of effort and gift. That the virtue of faith comes as a gift must never be used to excuse shoddy thinking or lack of discipline. Indeed, the conviction that God will give what God has promised frees us for profound effort. Whereas by God's grace faithful knowing is available to all, he gives it in greater measure to those who make the greater effort. Of all people, followers of Jesus Christ should be known for their discipline in and commitment to the practice of education. Moreover, this mysterious connection between our effort and God's gift prepares us to receive knowledge when it comes to us as God's gift.

One of the ways in which knowledge comes to us as a gift is friendship:

Whoever walks with the wise becomes wise,

but the companion of fools suffers harm. (Prov 13:20)

The relationship described here is much more than that of teacher-student; it is the relationship of friends.[23] Of course, discernment must be exercised, but the lesson of this passage and many others is that those who are teachers must seek also to befriend their students. If Jesus himself can call us "friends" (Jn 15:13-15), then those who are teachers can do no less.[24]

In the traditional, large classroom setting, however, this practice of friendship seems impossible. How does a teacher befriend so many different students? We who are teachers should, of course, seek to overcome the obstacles to friendship, but we can also look in another direction for our practice of education. Here the role of student peers is important. Time and again research has shown that other students are more determinative in the process of education than are teachers. If we are to make wise use of this knowledge, we must communicate the importance of friendship for the practice of education and encourage students to form their friendships accordingly. That in itself is an important accomplishment of the practice of education.

But the obstacles to education as a gift lie not only in our setting, they also lie within us. Since we have been taught by modernity to think that knowledge is an achievement of human powers, we think of education as an exercise in power. But if we understand that our knowing is formed by faith that comes to us as a gift in the disciple community, then we will be transformed so that we can practice education as a gift.[25]

As we learn this we will also learn that education is not a competition. Since we all, students and teachers alike, have been given the gift of the Holy Spirit, we will practice education that allows us to learn from each other. We will create a space within which the Holy Spirit teaches all of us through the gifts that we have all been given.[26]

Education as personal. In Proverbs we also have resources for the practice of education as personal.[27] In its use of various terms, Proverbs recognizes that students come to education with all their particularities.[28] First, there are the *prudent,* who are on the path of wisdom. Second are the *simple,* who are not on the path of wisdom and in danger of folly, yet who still can be taught. Third, there are the *fools,* who are well on their way down the path of folly but who may yet be rescued if they are subjected to strong discipline and correction. Finally there are the *scoffers,* who mistake folly for wisdom and wisdom for folly.

The recognition that students are formed in many different ways teaches us that our practice of education must be complex and marked by a practical wisdom that discerns the differences among students. The entire book of Proverbs is an extended lesson on this complexity and in this practice of discernment.

Even if we agree that the practice of education is more than the transference of knowledge from the teacher's mind to the student's, our traditional classroom setting resists the practice of education as personal. In large classes teaching must by necessity be largely impersonal. Responding appropriately to a wide range of students is difficult. Who are the prudent? the simple? the fools? the scoffers? In spite of the obstacles, teachers in whatever setting must seek to recognize the particularities of their students—they must approach them as persons.

I remember clearly an inattentive and seemingly resistant

student in one of my classes. When I responded to her in class, I usually treated her as a scoffer. Then I had an occasion to get to know her and discovered that her family situation at home was a source of enormous stress. Of course, my responses to her changed dramatically after that conversation.

Unfortunately, teachers do not always have the opportunity to get to know students, nor are all students as forthcoming as that one. Nevertheless, if our practice of education seeks to form the virtue of faith as personal, teachers must be committed to their students as persons. Moreover, for our practice of education to be personal, we must recognize that teachers are persons. If teachers are to habituate students in the virtue of faith, they must be willing to be persons who are themselves being formed in faith and who bring that virtue to the practice of education. Education can be "practiced" only by those who are themselves willing to participate in the practice and be transformed by it.

We who are teachers must ourselves be habituated in faith before we can give to others. In our "horror of self-encounter" we who are teachers refuse to acknowledge that what we know has been given to us.[29] We prefer to masquerade as self-sufficient individuals who have achieved knowledge by our own efforts. To acknowledge that we must be transformed entails a self-encounter from which our knowledge protects us. If our practice of education is to be personal, we who are teachers must learn that our knowing, our very lives, are given to us in Christ.

In the end, Thomas Howard also realized that our knowing is rooted in Jesus Christ:

> In the figure of Jesus we saw Immanuel, that is, God, that is, Love. It was a figure who appearing inauspiciously among us, broke up our secularist and our religious categories and beckoned us and judged us and damned us and saved us and exhibited to us a kind of life that participates in the indestructible. And it was a figure who announced the validity of our eternal effort to discover significance and beauty beyond

inanition and horror by announcing to us the unthinkable: redemption.[30]

This vision is the basis of faith as the Christian way of knowing, and it gives direction to our eschatological practice of education.

The Eschaton of Education

I have suggested some ways in which the practice of education forms the virtue of faith. Now I will approach the practice of education from another angle, namely, the direction given to our practice of education by Christian convictions about "the good life," summarized in the term *eschaton*. Remember, *eschaton* is the way Christians construe the *telos* of humanity. Christians believe that the good toward which all of reality is oriented is God's redemption of creation in Jesus Christ. For Christians then the good encompasses more than humankind: it embraces all creation. Therefore the good life for the disciple community is the life that is formed by the eschatological promise of the redemption of creation.

This concern recovers one additional aspect of faith as personal that I have not yet considered—the virtue of faith shaped by the person of Jesus Christ. We return to the person of Jesus Christ here because, for the church, Jesus Christ is the revelation and the enactment of the eschaton, God's redemption of creation. As we will see more fully in the next chapter, Jesus Christ is the revelation of the world's future. Moreover, to the extent that Christ rules in our world today, that future is present.

Blessed misfits. As I consider how the eschaton should shape our present practice of education, I will argue that the practice of education should produce not "well-adjusted misfits" but "blessed misfits."[31] This phrase neatly captures an eschatological practice of education. If we are being formed for a world redeemed by God, then we will indeed be misfits in a world not yet fully redeemed. But if the redemption of the world is indeed the truth, then to live in the light of that redemption is to be blessed. Moreover, if the eschaton is the work of God and not of humanity, then *blessed* is a better term than *well-adjusted*. Blessedness is a gift, not an achievement.

A classic description of blessed misfits is found in the beatitudes of Jesus' Sermon on the Mount:

> Blessed are the poor in spirit, for theirs is the kingdom of heaven.
>
> Blessed are those who mourn, for they will be comforted.
>
> Blessed are the meek, for they will inherit the earth.
>
> Blessed are those who hunger and thirst for righteousness, for they will be filled.
>
> Blessed are the merciful, for they will receive mercy.
>
> Blessed are the pure in heart, for they will see God.
>
> Blessed are the peacemakers, for they will be called children of God.
>
> Blessed are those who are persecuted for righteousness' sake, for theirs is the kingdom of heaven.
>
> Blessed are you when people revile you and persecute you and utter all kinds of evil against you falsely on my account. Rejoice and be glad, for your reward is great in heaven, for in the same way they persecuted the prophets who were before you. (Mt 5:3-12)

In this passage Jesus describes those formed in faith by his education as blessed, but he connects their blessedness with an unusual series of characterizations. Those who are poor in spirit, who mourn, who are meek and so on—these are the blessed.

We do not usually think of blessedness in such terms. Can you imagine a Christian college telling prospective students, "If you come to our college, you will be taught to be poor in spirit, to mourn, to be meek, to be hungry and thirsty, and to be persecuted"? Yet that is how Jesus identified those who are blessed.

Such an identification makes sense only if we recognize that Jesus is describing a practice of education that habituates disciples in faith and in the life of the kingdom of heaven. Since such a life is oriented toward God's eschatological redemption of creation, it is, even now, a blessed life in the kingdom, one that looks forward to being comforted, inheriting the earth, being filled, receiving mercy, seeing God and being called the children of God.

If our practice of education habituates us in this faith, it will also teach us to be poor in spirit as we come to see how far the world is from the kingdom. It will teach us to mourn the brokenness in the world and in our lives. It will teach us to be meek as we realize that all we have is a gift from God. As our practice of education forms in us the blessedness of faith, it will at the same time misfit us for the world.

In MacIntyre's terms, Jesus' beatitudes identify goods that are internal rather than external to the practice of education. Jesus does not instruct us to become poor in spirit, mournful, hungry and persecuted. We do not become those things in order to be blessed. Rather, they are simply marks of life oriented toward God's eschatological redemption. These characteristics are integral to our being habituated in faith by our practice of education, and at the same time we will be blessed.

We typically seek education in order to realize external goods. For example, we ask, "Will this education make me more successful, more employable, more desirable?" But those are the wrong kinds of questions to ask, and orienting education as a response to those kinds of questions distorts our practice of education. What we must ask instead is this: "Does our practice of education participate in God's work of redemption, habituate us in that work and extend our ability to participate in God's work of redemption?" In asking this question we incorporate all of the marks of the virtue of faith because God's work of redemption is cosmic, it is a gift, it is communal, and it is personal.

Misfits in the world. In our cultural situation our practice of education must continue to make us "blessed misfits." We will be blessed as our practice of education forms faith in us, but we will be misfit for the world in two ways.[32]

First, we will be misfit for a world marked by *secularism*. As we have already seen at length, this secularism is characteristic of modernity as it places boundaries around faith and the sacred. If our practice of education is formed in faith, we will be misfits who recognize no boundaries to God's rule, what we know in Christ or our practice of education.

Second, we will be misfit for a world marked by *pluralism*. In one sense pluralism is simply a fact—people believe many different things. But pluralism is also more—it is the belief that there are many "truths," that truth is fragmented, that there is no One God and that we should simply tolerate each other's "truths." The early Christians lived in such a world, a world marked by belief in many gods. The Athenians, with their desire to tolerate all gods (Acts 17:16-34), are a wonderful example of pluralism. But the early church did not accept this pluralism, and neither should we. The virtue of faith as I have described it stands against pluralism. Our practice of education must enable us to see through pluralism to the reconciliation of all things in Christ.

Misfits in the church. Now to a more disquieting suggestion: Shouldn't an eschatological practice of education extend even to misfitting us for the church? Here we encounter serious danger of misunderstanding. The purpose of a faithful practice of education is not to alienate us from the church and the gospel. Rather, the faithful practice of education should teach us to love the church as the people called by God to witness to the good news of God's work of redemption, which is greater than the church. The purpose of the church is not to witness to itself but to witness to the work of God in Christ. To use Jesus' terms, the church is witness to the kingdom of God. Our practice of education must habituate us in the kingdom and habituate a desire for more faithful witness to that kingdom on the part of the church.

In this sense we will become misfits in the church, never comfortable, always knowing there is distance between the church and the kingdom, always on guard against the corruption and distortion which our unacknowledged, unconfessed sin introduces into our endeavors.[34] Since the church is not the kingdom, education that is Christian will misfit people for the church. It will form in them a love for the kingdom that becomes a commitment to the church as witness to the kingdom. But since they will recognize the distance between the church and the kingdom, they will be misfits in the church in at least two ways.

First, they will be misfit for a church that seeks to rule the world.[35] Confusing the kingdom and the church, many contemporary Christians believe that we are placed in the world to rule. (This can be true of both the liberal and the conservative church.) Much of our education reflects and reinforces the conviction that we are to rule the world. For example, we tell students considering a college that if they really want success, power and money in the world, then they should get the best education available to them, given their intellectual and financial resources—and we measure "best" in worldly terms.

When we continue our education as adults, it is usually to know more, to increase our employability, to become happier, healthier people. Even the educational practices of the church may be promoted as producing happier, more effective people for this world. Stories of success produced by Christian education, resulting in a fast-track career or a quick climb up the ladder, have no relation to Jesus' description of the kind of people who habitually follow him.

If we took Jesus' words seriously, how would we evaluate education? Here is what he says: If any among you would be great, they must become least of all and servant of all (Mk 10:42-45). Have you ever heard anyone say that they are attending a particular college or class or acquiring a particular skill or attending a particular church in order to become more humble, poor in spirit or hungry for righteousness? That is what our practice of education should aim at—not turning individuals into lords but into servants, not producing people who have increased control of their lives but people who have increased their ability to give up their lives for the gospel.

Faith teaches that life and knowledge are a gift. If God does not impose faith upon us but offers it freely as a gift, then we who are formed in the virtue of faith will not seek to impose our rule on the world. On the contrary we will serve the world by offering faith in the gospel as a gift to be accepted. We are free to serve as we are habituated in faith in the One who is among us as servant. We are free to give away knowledge, not hoard it and protect it as a power-play as we are educated in the faith that is God's gift to us in Jesus Christ. We will offer that gift to others with integrity and persuasiveness as we are formed by our education into blessed misfits.

The second characteristic of the church for which we will be misfit is the desire of many for absolute certainty and truth. In reaction against the pluralism of the world, many in the church emphasize the importance of absolute truth. Dissatisfied with relativism and an individualism that views opinion as knowledge, many seek truth that is absolute and certain. The church is right to resist the pluralism and relativism of today's culture, but we must recognize that the quest for absolute certainty and truth is itself a product of modernity. Moreover, this quest will return to the relativism of today, because modernity's criteria for certainty and truth cannot be met.

"Blessed misfits" who have been formed in faith will resist pluralism and relativism not by seeking absolute certainty and truth but by seeking Jesus Christ. They will remember that the virtue of faith begins in the gift of a relationship to Jesus Christ. Faith is the habitual following of Jesus Christ in all areas of our lives. Knowledge rooted in this faith is personal knowledge. Personal knowledge, relational knowledge, is never absolute and certain.

Certainly our knowing formed by faith is dependable—first, because the One through whom we know is unchanging, and second, because our knowledge is rooted in the gift of God that will never be taken away. Yet by its very nature, personal knowledge is open-ended and incomplete. That is why the Christian life is a pilgrimage, and why Christians are disciples—learners, not masters.

When we in the church seek "absolute certainty and truth," we are succumbing to the modernist quest for mastery and control. At its worst, our desire to have the absolute truth leaves others outside faith through our faithless attempts to control access to the knowledge of faith. We want to be dispensers of knowledge, and we want others to be consumers who are dependent on us for their supply of truth.

In contrast, following Jesus Christ is a process of giving up control and showing others the way to personal knowledge of Jesus Christ. If we are to be formed as people of faith who are fit for the kingdom and misfit for a church that is captive to modernity, then we must be concerned to school people in discipleship.[35] We are all learners in the church, but our task is to cultivate the disciplines that sustain followers of Jesus Christ, not to master absolute truth. We must learn that if faith is the Christian way of knowing and a gift from God, then not having the answers is not failure but witness, a pointing beyond ourselves to the God who loves us in our finitude and forgives us in our failure.

People who are educated in the virtue of faith will be able to sustain discipleship when there are no answers because they know that God is trustworthy and faithful. People who are not habituated into this faith have to have answers in order to continue. Their discipleship is based on their power and control, not on trust in Jesus Christ.

Thus the practice of education that forms faith makes us "blessed misfits," blessed by our participation in God's redemption, misfit for all that is not yet redeemed. Such a practice is impossible in our own strength—it is possible only with the power of God at work in us. That power is the work of the risen Lord among us through the presence of the Holy Spirit. That is why followers of Jesus Christ seek not a *method* but a *practice* of education.

Conclusion

How should the Neal family select a college? I have not answered that question for them, but I have given the criteria by which they should decide and by which we may pursue the practice of education in the whole of life. Education that habituates us in faith recognizes the rule of God over the entire cosmos. It recognizes faith and all of our knowing as a gift that comes through the gospel of Jesus Christ. It is practiced in the Spirit-gifted community. It responds to us in our particularities as persons. And it educates us as blessed misfits in the life of the kingdom, which is the redemption of all creation. That is the gospel-shaped practice of education that habituates us in faith as the Christian way of knowing.

Five

HOPE AND THE
CHRISTIAN WAY
OF BEING

· · · · · · · · · · · · · · · · · · · ·

R̲ECENTLY I RECEIVED AN INVITATION TO SUBSCRIBE TO A NEW
magazine. Introduced as a "magazine that will make you feel
better about the world, alter the way you see it, and open your
eyes to inspiring people already changing it," *Hope* magazine
promised to be "a new celebration of the human spirit at its best"
and a guide to "*the power of human intervention.*" The publica-
tion of this magazine represents the desperation of our search
for hope, for if we had it, we wouldn't have to publish a magazine
about it.

We are desperate for hope because all the old sources of hope
are crumbling. The Marxist hope has faded, and even democratic
capitalism shows many signs of instability. Unemployment, racial
conflict, uncontrollable violence, drug use and moral decay are
threats that we cannot deny. In the midst of these things, the
abandonment of hope may seem to be the most realistic response.

How can we recover the hope that our world so desperately

needs? Should we "feel better about the world"? Is hope grounded in "the human spirit" and in "the power of human intervention"? Does hope sustain us by giving us an alternative to "the world"? Is hope grounded in the human spirit and human powers, or is it grounded in the Holy Spirit and the work of God?

In this chapter I will describe the virtue of hope that is inculcated by the gospel of Jesus Christ. In a world filled with illusions of hope that capture us and distort our lives, the only real hope is the coming of God in Jesus Christ. In a world tempted by the abandonment of hope, the only sure foundation of hope is God's eschatological redemption. We must be habituated in the hope of the gospel if we are to discern illusory hopes and witness faithfully to the only hope of the world—Jesus Christ.

Hope is the virtue that best describes the Christian *way of being*. Although hope is a familiar concept, *way of being* may sound strange. *Way of being* refers to how we live in the light of how we view reality. For instance, a way of being is represented by the old, familiar bumper sticker "He who dies with the most toys wins." The person who displays this bumper sticker clearly has a view of reality that guides a way of life. Likewise, the rejoinder "He who dies with the most toys still dies" represents a view of reality and a way of life. Perhaps the Christian way of being cannot be reduced to a bumper sticker slogan, but understood in the light of the gospel, the Christian way of being is accurately represented by the virtue of "hope in Jesus Christ."

This virtue was clearly represented by my father as he was dying in December 1994. When my family was able to join him and my mother and my sister's family in Oklahoma, his doctors had just proposed surgery. But they warned him that he had only a 50 percent chance of surviving the surgery. His response was "Either way, I win." However, as his health worsened, the surgery was canceled, and we all prepared for his death.

As his passing grew nearer and all thought of "the power of human intervention" came to an end, my father's hope grew stronger and more palpable. None of us "felt better about a world" in which dying was causing pain and in which death would soon cause separation, but we all had *hope* in the redemption of Jesus Christ. As we will see later in this chapter, that hope made all the difference in my father's dying (see 1 Cor 15).

Since the gospel is determinative for our account of the virtue of hope, I will begin by considering hope as a virtue rooted in the gospel of Jesus Christ. Then I will examine our cultural situation to see why we need the virtue of hope. Finally I will give an account of the virtue of hope as it shapes the Christian way of being.

Hope as a Virtue

When we speak of "the Christian hope" we typically refer to the return of Christ and the events surrounding his return. This eschatological emphasis was the mark of Christianity in the early centuries and has been a distinguishing characteristic of evangelical Christianity for the past century. Differences on particular details, however, have at times created thin but deep divides even among evangelicals.[1] I intend to develop an account of hope as a virtue that does not presuppose a particular eschatological scheme. I will argue simply that the virtue of hope identifies the way Christians wait for the redemption of creation.

We spend a lot of time waiting. But *how* we wait depends on what we are waiting for. If we are waiting for the results of medical tests, our waiting may take on uncomfortable characteristics. If we are waiting for a bonus check from our employer or a refund from the IRS, our waiting takes on very different characteristics.

One of the determinative characteristics of our lives as Christians is that we are waiting for the redemption that has been accomplished in Jesus Christ. Our life as the disciple community is stretched between the first coming of God in Christ and his second coming. In between these times the gospel calls us to live in hope. In this sense hope is not the content of an eschatological scheme but the way we live in light of the eschaton.

Hope as a way of life is best identified through the language of virtue. Hope becomes the habitual way of life for those who see their lives stretched between Christ's first and second coming. As a Christian virtue, hope finds its identity in the living tradition of the gospel and is determined by the particular *telos*—the eschaton of the gospel. This means that hope is grounded in God, not in humankind. As a Christian virtue, hope shapes and is shaped by the gospel, not by the world. As we will see in the next chapter, hope as a virtue forms and is formed by Christian practice.

Why We Need the Virtue of Hope

Since hope as a virtue is grounded in God and not in humanity, it exposes the illusory ways that people seek to ground hope. These illusions are rampant in our culture, but they have also penetrated the church. As these illusions have become exposed for what they are, our culture has had no place to turn for hope. As a result, we live in a world marked largely by hopelessness.

Hope in modernity. Our culture sustained the illusion of hope for a long period of time through an optimistic belief in human progress; some still cling to it. This doctrine of progress has had many supposed foundations. The rationalism of the Enlightenment was supposed to have ended the horrendous wars that convulsed Europe in the seventeenth century. The rise of democracy seemed to free humanity from the political chains that enslaved it. Modern medicine promised the end of the plagues that had devastated Europe. Industrialization expected to free humankind from the drudgery of manual labor.

Yet in the twentieth century, rational, democratic Europe fought the bloodiest wars in history. Even though medicine has extended life, it does not have the power to make people morally better or to prevent death. At the end of the twentieth century some foolishly hail technology as the new source of hope.[2]

All these attempts to ground hope are bound to fail, because all make the same mistake: they seek to ground hope in human achievement. Even pessimism, the typical immediate response to disillusionment, makes this mistake. Optimism says that the future lies within the power of humanity and the future looks good. Pessimism says that the future lies within the power of humanity and the future looks bad. Both optimism and pessimism are products of modernity, with its belief that only humans may control the future. One view connects human control to an optimistic view of human nature, the other to a pessimistic view of human nature.

Cynicism in postmodernity. Over the past several decades much of our culture has abandoned the optimism and pessimism of modernity in favor of a third response—cynicism. Cynicism says that we have no control over the future and that we cannot really know what the future holds. This cynicism is one of the marks of postmodernity and is exemplified among postmodernists in a variety of ways. Some of their arguments are helpful in exposing the illusory hopes of modernity, but I want to go beyond postmodernity to offer an alternative to cynicism, one that is found in the virtue of hope.

One expression of postmodern cynicism is its attack on metaphysics and ontology, the philosophical disciplines that seek to describe reality and being. Since this attack is complex, I cannot explore it fully here.[3] However, I can note that this postmodernist critique has effectively exposed the illusion of grounding hope in human reason. It serves as a warning that the virtue of hope must be grounded in God's revelation, not human reason. Of course, such an account of hope will not convince many—perhaps most—postmodernists. My point is that the postmodernist critique does not attack faithful practice of the gospel, it attacks the illusory products of human reason.

Another expression of postmodernist cynicism that follows from the first is the practice of deconstruction. Deconstruction is another complex phenomenon that I cannot explore fully here. But note that deconstruction is, in at least one sense, the exposure of the illusions that we humans "construct." Deconstruction simply seeks to show that the foundations that supposedly support human life are themselves simply the products of human life. So they are no foundations at all.

When applied to the stories we tell, deconstruction again simply seeks to expose those narratives as stories that we have constructed to legitimate or extend our power. The deepest suspicion is directed toward *metanarratives,* stories that purport to incorporate our lives in all reality. Examples of metanarrative include ideologies such as Marxism and democratic capitalism, philosophies such as idealism, personalism and existentialism, and religions.[4] According to postmodernism these metanarratives disguise the human condition and represent the worst kind of totalitarianism.

In the end, cynicism is a virtue produced by modernity that has become characteristic of much postmodernism. Cynicism is the way we protect ourselves when we think that we have no one to depend on but ourselves. It is our way of making ourselves appear superior to "all those poor people who actually believe something." Ultimately cynicism makes us more susceptible to lies because it is grounded in the lie that there is nothing to believe in. Believing this lie, we become habituated to believing lies.[5]

The temptations of modernity and postmodernity. In this cultural situation the church is greatly tempted to support the claims of modernity. The church has lived with modernity for a long time and has worked out responses to the questions of modernity. The church has a history that, at its best, guides our witness to modernity, so we are comfortable with it. Moreover, postmodernity represents social upheaval and cultural uncertainty. Since the church has lived with modernity for so long and has in many instances identified success with modernist culture, the church may naturally resist postmodernity in the name of social order and cultural stability that will also ensure its survival. However, modernity is not the gospel and the survival of the church is not dependent on social conditions or cultural circumstances. For the church to support modernity would be a betrayal of the gospel of hope.

We in the church have been co-opted by modernist illusions and the postmodernist exposure of these illusions whenever we talk and act as if our present lives and the future lie within our control. We can briefly (and risking some misunderstanding) express what the gospel calls the church to by saying that the church should live as if daring God to allow the church to disappear. No, in reality we, the church, should continually "give up our lives" for the sake of the gospel, knowing that if we seek, as the disciple community, to save our lives we will lose them. Only by giving up our lives for Christ will we find them.

Yet how hard it is for us to do this. We are still captive in many ways to the illusions of modernity. When we present the gospel as a means to greater control of our lives, we have been captured by the illusions of modernity. When we plot the survival of the church, we are seeking to save our lives. When we think that the church is something to "manage," we seek to save our lives. When we market the church, we are captive to the illusions of modernity. Only as we recover the virtue of hope can we find our life as a church and witness faithfully to the gospel in a culture marked by the illusions of modernity and the cynicism of postmodernity.

At the same time that we are drawn to modernity, we may be increasingly tempted to support postmodernity. We may turn to postmodernity as an ally as we recognize the church's complicity with modernity and the power of the postmodern critique. Sensitive to the postmodern critique of totalitarianism, we may recognize the church's guilt and affirm the claims of postmodernity. Although there is truth in these responses, we must also discern the difference between modernity and the gospel, between the church's faithless and faithful witness.

In this task of discernment postmodernity is an ally—or perhaps better, a helpful critic—but it is not an entirely benign ally nor is it an unproblematic critic. Postmodernity, adopted uncritically by the church, would lead to an abandonment of the gospel. Over against postmodernity's "incredulity toward metanarratives" (Lyotard), the church sets the gospel as a different kind of metanarrative.

The gospel is a metanarrative—it is about all of reality. But it is a metanarrative different from the metanarratives of modernity. The gospel is a metanarrative rooted in God's revelation, not in human reason. As such the gospel calls us to serve, not to rule, to witness, not to coerce. Over against the will to power and violence enshrined by postmodernity, the church sets the gospel as the story of God's reconciliation of all things through the violence inflicted on Jesus Christ.[6] The gospel is the story not of the human overcoming of violence but of God's overcoming of violence to which we witness through the virtue of hope.

The church is co-opted by postmodernity and betrays the gospel when we simply accept the postmodern critique and commit ourselves to the will to power. The church seldom, if ever, explicitly adopts postmodern cynicism, but we adopt it implicitly in two ways: we adopt the postmodern will to power whenever we succumb to the "Constantinian temptation" to rule the world through human effort;[7] we adopt the cynicism of postmodernity whenever we succumb to the "relativist temptation" to abandon the cosmic scope of the gospel.

At a deeper level, we can use the language of being to describe our cultural situation. Modernity's anxiety about being—that is, anxiety about the foundations for the continuing existence of humankind—leads to human efforts to ground our being. Those efforts lead fallen humanity inevitably to violence. Postmodernity's inevitable violence becomes the mark of humankind and leads to the conviction that violence is the nature of being. In theological language we can say that modernity seeks salvation through human effort and that postmodernity abandons the quest for salvation and accepts our damnation. Over against these illusions—that we must achieve our salvation and that there is no salvation—stands the hope of the gospel.[8]

The Virtue of Hope and the Christian Way of Being
Now we turn to an account of the virtue of hope that will help enable faithful witness to the gospel in our cultural situation. In the midst of many temptations this account must be rooted in the gospel. We cannot simply add hope to our cultural situation, we must rebuild our understanding of reality on the foundation of the gospel of Jesus Christ. As Jacques Ellul reminds us, "The hope of Jesus Christ is never a dash of pepper or a spoonful of mustard. It is bread and wine, the essential and basic food itself, without which there is only the delirium of knowledge and the illusion of action. It is essential that hope be the all."[9]

Only habituation in the virtue of hope will enable witness to the gospel in the midst of optimism, pessimism and cynicism. In order to give an account of habituation in the virtue of hope, I will examine hope as eschatological, personal, communal and cosmic.

Hope as eschatological. The virtue of hope is determined by its eschaton—an admittedly awkward use of the term that reminds us of the gospel's transformation of the notion of *telos.* For the disciple community the eschaton is the redemption of creation accomplished and revealed in Jesus Christ. This creates a special situation for Christians. The eschaton is not simply something to which we look forward. We also look to the past, where this redemption is accomplished and revealed in the life, death and resurrection of Jesus Christ. And we look to the present, where this eschaton is at work and is guaranteed by the power of the Holy Spirit.

This means that Christians have a peculiar understanding of history. History progresses, but its progress is not linear. We cannot plot on a line where we are in relation to "the beginning and end" of history. Rather than progressing linearly, history progresses eschatologically, which means that the progress of history is marked by our participation in the work of redemption, not by a chain of cause and effect. History has a goal, but that goal is not the last point in a line that ends history.[10] Rather, the goal of history is eschatological, the coming of God in Christ that renders history supremely meaningful through redemption.[11] History has meaning, but that meaning is not achieved or constructed by humanity, it is given by God in Christ.

This eschatological view of history determines the virtue of hope. The virtue of hope is not produced by figuring out how close we are to the end or by analyzing the outcome of a line of cause and effect and proving that the outcome is good. Nor is hope produced by projecting human desires into the future and then reading them back into the present. Hope is grounded in our knowledge of God's work of redemption in Christ.

At the same time that our eschatological view of history forms hope, it effectively denies human control of history and hope. Like faith, hope comes to us as a gift. The virtue of hope is shaped not by human effort or by human construction but by God's action in Jesus Christ. From this action we know what gives history meaning and we know where it is headed, but we cannot ourselves give meaning to history nor can we steer history toward its destiny.

As my father lay dying, his hope and our hope did not depend on human control of his situation, nor did it depend on some special insight that we had into how soon history would end. Rather, our hope was grounded in our trust in the redemption that God has accomplished in Jesus Christ. As my father's death grew nearer, his hope grew stronger because it was grounded in God's power, not in my father's.

Like faith, the virtue of hope is present today in the gift of the Holy Spirit. Through this gift, God's eschatological work of redemption is present. But this work of redemption is not yet complete. As Paul describes the redemption of creation for which we long, he reminds us that

> not only the creation, but we ourselves, who have the first fruits of the Spirit, groan inwardly while we wait for adoption, the redemption of our bodies. For in hope we were saved. Now hope that is seen is not hope. For who hopes for what is seen? But if we hope for what we do not see, we wait for it with patience. (Rom 8:23-25)

Today the world is not yet fully redeemed. We must acknowledge that the world is still in rebellion against God when it seeks to accomplish its own salvation and when it abandons the hope of salvation. Yet the work of redemption does go on. When, by faith, we come to see God's judgment in the midst of the violence and cynicism, God is acting redemptively. When, by faith, we come to know and participate in God's reconciliation of all things in Christ, God is acting redemptively. So through the gift of the Holy Spirit we are stretched between the eschaton that has come and is still coming, and so we live by the virtue of hope grounded in the knowledge of faith.[12]

The virtue of hope that is shaped eschatologically has a number of characteristics. First, hope is the virtue of a people who are "on the way."[13] Hope marks the habituation of lives that know their destination but have not yet arrived. Second, hope is a virtue marked by peaceableness. Knowing that our being and future are established in Jesus Christ and guaranteed by the gift of the Holy Spirit, the disciple community has no need to strive for salvation. There is nothing to fight for, we have only to receive. Third, hope is a virtue marked by patience. We who live eschatologically know that God's work of redemption is still coming. Since we are already participants in that work of redemption by the power of the Holy Spirit, the virtue of hope is not passivity opposed to activity but patience opposed to anxiety. Patience is the mark of our activity, not our inactivity.[14] Finally, hope is a virtue marked by righteousness. Since the eschaton brings righteousness, those who live in hope will also live in righteousness.[15]

Being as eschatological. An eschatologically determined hope gives direction to the Christian way of being in the midst of our cultural situation. As we are habituated as "a people on the way," who have not yet arrived, we live as people who are dependent, not independent. Against the optimistic, and sometimes pessimistic, self-sufficiency of modernity, we witness to the all-sufficiency of God. Against the cynical self-effacement of postmodernity, we affirm that we are on the way to finding ourselves in Christ even as we deny ourselves.

As we are habituated into the peaceableness that comes from the gift of hope, we cease our striving against one another. Against the unceasing conflict that marks modernity's quest to achieve certainty of being, hope witnesses to the assurance of being that comes as a gift. Against the cynical and nihilistic violence of postmodernity, hope witnesses to the transformation of our violent being through God's reconciliation of all things in Christ. Since our being and our future are given by God, we who hope in Christ have no need to protect our being through violent resistance against the forces of nothingness. The threat of non-being has been overcome through the gift of God in Jesus Christ.

As we are habituated in the virtue of hope, we endure with patience the suffering that comes from living in a time when the eschaton is still coming.[16] Since God's work of redemption is not yet complete, we cannot give a complete account of the meaning of history and of suffering. But we know that history, including suffering, has been given meaning through the death and resurrection of Jesus Christ.[17] Against the striving of modernity that

seeks to give meaning to history through human achievement
that only leads to further suffering, hope waits patiently for the
coming of God that transforms suffering and gives meaning to
history. Against the cynicism of postmodernity that in effect
simply accepts suffering as the meaninglessness of history, hope
patiently witnesses to the end of suffering and the meaningful-
ness of history brought by the coming of God.[18]

As we are habituated in the virtue of hope, we live in the
righteousness of the eschaton. Since the patience of hope teaches
endurance in suffering, we may wrongly conclude that hope is
unconcerned with unrighteousness and injustice in the world
because the eschaton of righteousness is yet to come. But that
conclusion mistakes the character of patience and of eschatological righteousness and justice. Patience for the disciple community
is not the acceptance of suffering and meaninglessness but the
way of waiting for the coming of God that transforms suffering
and redeems history.

For the disciple community, therefore, hope is habituated
through patiently living today in the light of the eschaton that is
still coming. It is patience in doing the works of God. Therefore
patience actually strengthens the claims of righteousness and
justice because it is the way the disciple community lives in the
eschaton today.

So the virtue of hope habituates us in righteousness. Against
the attempts of modernity to establish "righteousness," to justify
our lives through human effort alone, hope inculcates a righteousness that comes as God's gift. Against the conviction of
postmodernity that humans are incapable of righteousness, that
our lives cannot be justified and that righteousness is absent from
this world, hope teaches that righteousness and justification come
as a gift of God and that righteousness is present, though not yet
fully present, in this world. As the disciple community then,
stretched between the revelation of God's righteousness in Jesus
Christ and the completion of that righteousness, we live in hope

through the power of the Holy Spirit.[19]

Hope as personal. In addition to being eschatological, the virtue of hope is personal in two ways. First, its ground and goal is the person of Jesus Christ. Since this characteristic overlaps significantly with hope as eschatological, we will not need to consider it at length. What we do need to do is to make more explicit connection between Jesus Christ and some of the points made in the previous section.

In the person of Jesus Christ the eschaton is established and revealed. In his identity as fully human, fully divine, Jesus Christ makes actual and available the hope that is God's gift. As human, Jesus Christ lives in hope. As God, he brings the eschaton.

In his life Jesus Christ enacts the hope in which his followers are formed. In particular, the virtue of hope is embodied in his great act of self-giving in washing the feet of the disciples. As John introduces the act, he tells us that "during supper Jesus, knowing that the Father had given all things into his hands, *and that he had come from God and was going to God,* got up from the table, took off his outer robe, and tied a towel around himself" (Jn 13:2-5, italics added). Later we are given these words of instruction from Jesus: "So if I, your Lord and Teacher, have washed your feet, you also ought to wash one another's feet" (13:14).

In this act our Lord and Teacher Jesus Christ calls into question, indeed overturns, all our illusions about world mastery. Furthermore, his act and our hope have the same foundation. He knew "that he had come from God and was going to God," and this knowledge enabled him to surrender his role as Master in order to become Servant. Likewise hope, through which we know that our being comes from God and is going to God, enables us to surrender our quest for world mastery in order to become servants.

In his death and resurrection Jesus Christ embodies the hope in which we live. In his death Jesus confronted the great enemy of being and of the future, for death seems to be the end of being and the cancellation of the future. In his willing endurance of death, Jesus did not meet the apparent power of nonbeing with a violence of his own that sought to counter it. Such a response would only add to the apparent power of nonbeing. Instead, Jesus faced death with hope. And his hope was not disappointed, for his resurrection declared the power of God over death and nonbeing for all who live in the hope of the gospel.

If this is the hope revealed in the person of Christ, then the virtue of hope is also personal in its transformation of all who are in Christ. Hope is not something outside persons, hope is the transformation of our very being into new being. In Christ this new being is enabled to live in hope rather than in the illusion of hope. Our new being not only comes from God but is also going to God. In Christ we are habituated as servants rather than masters. In Christ our new being is habituated in peaceableness, not violence. Assured of our being in God, we no longer need violence to assert our being against the apparent forces of nonbeing. These changes in us are not merely an improvement in who we are, they are a transformation of who we are—in Christ we are new persons who live by hope.[20]

Although this process of transformation was incomplete in my father's life (as it is in all of us), the virtue of hope was nevertheless very evident. During almost fifty years of ministry my father had been an evangelist, a pastor, a professor and a missions administrator. Deeply suspicious of the worth of his own efforts and always thinking that he could have done more, he knew that his hope was in Jesus Christ, not his own efforts. As a result of that knowledge and of the peaceableness that he achieved only through submitting himself to God's discipline, he did not respond violently to the many attacks that were directed toward his ministry throughout the years. His hope was not in the rightness of his own actions but in the righteousness of God that comes to us in the gift of Jesus Christ.

Being as personal. Hope as personal has obvious implications for our way of being in the world. Hope that is rooted in the person of Jesus Christ exposes the illusions and errors of modernity and postmodernity. Against the illusory hope of modernity that is grounded in human ability and achievement, hope witnesses to Jesus Christ as its only foundation. Against the illusory hopelessness of postmodernity, hope witnesses to the presence of Jesus Christ, whose work is not yet complete.

The virtue of hope as the transformation of persons in Jesus Christ establishes a way of living counter to the violence of modernity and postmodernity. Habituated in the self-giving servanthood of Jesus Christ, we turn from modernity's quest for mastery and postmodernity's will to power. Since our self-giving is rooted in Christ, it results not in our nonbeing but in our being: "Those who find their life will lose it, and those who lose their life for my sake will find it" (Mt 10:39).

Finally the virtue of hope that is formed by Christ's death and resurrection transforms our being from violence to peaceableness. Throughout the centuries followers of Jesus Christ have literally lost their lives for Christ's sake by refusing to meet violence with violence. The violence that is rooted in the fear of nonbeing has no place in the virtue of hope. Through habituation in hope the disciple community knows the gospel as something for which to suffer and die, but not for which to kill. To kill for the gospel is a denial of the gift of being that comes in the person of Jesus Christ.

That we have so often been willing to kill in the name of Christ is a sign of our cultural corruption. As we are formed in and transformed by the virtue of hope, we will be enabled by the Spirit to discern our captivity to our cultural situation and to participate in the peaceableness of the gospel. In a world marked by the violent mastery characteristic of modernity and the violent will to power characteristic of postmodernity, faithful witness to the gospel depends on the virtue of hope that builds on the foundation of Jesus Christ and transforms us.

Hope as communal. Since the turn to virtue is a turn from the individual to the community, one of the marks of the virtue of hope is that it is communal.[21] However, to say simply that hope is communal is insufficient and misleading because the character of any virtue is largely determined by the particular community within which it takes shape. So what we must do in this section is attend to the church—the disciple community—and the ways that it is formed by and forms the hope of the gospel.

Since Jesus Christ is known as our hope only in the gospel, the virtue of hope can be learned only in the disciple community through which Christ is known. Moreover, since hope is one mark of the transformation of our being into new being, hope can be a virtue only within the new community, the church. In this sense the church is a community that owes its existence to God and to no other power. Once we were not a people, now we are a people (1 Pet 2:10, drawing on Hos 2:23). Hope then is the mark of this community and no other.

But we must be careful. Jesus Christ is "the hope of the world," but here hope describes the power by which the world is transformed, not something that the world can possess as the world. In other words, Jesus Christ is the only hope for the salvation of the world, but only the disciple community knows this hope. We can take this one step further by saying that the only way for the world to know that its hope is salvation in Jesus Christ is through the life of the church as witness to hope. This witness invites the world to give up its illusions of hope and be transformed by the gospel.

In the disciple community the virtue of hope is formed as we learn to live peaceably with each other. In his letter to the Ephesians Paul describes this clearly. After identifying the basic division of humanity in the ancient world, at least from the Jewish perspective, as the division between Jew and Gentile, Paul describes the unity worked by the gospel:

> For [Christ Jesus] is our peace; in his flesh he has made both groups into one and has broken down the dividing wall, that is, the hostility between us. He has abolished the law with its commandments and ordinances, that he might create in himself one new humanity in place of the two, thus making peace, and might reconcile both groups to God in one body through the cross, thus putting to death that hostility through it. (Eph 2:14-16)

The church then, as one new humanity, is a sign in the present of the eschaton that is still coming.

In this community we are habituated in the peaceableness of hope as the difference and division that marks the human condition is overcome by the work of God in Christ through the power of the Holy Spirit. That can happen only as we are made new beings and new humanity through the gift of God. Through this transformation our differences become gifts for one another that together enable us to grow up into Christ (1 Cor 12; Eph 4:1-16).

In the disciple community we are called to the righteousness that marks the virtue of hope. Since this righteousness is the righteousness of those who hope in Christ, the world cannot be made righteous as the world. The calling of the church then is to live itself in the righteousness of the eschaton, not to make the world righteous. Since the world is in rebellion against God, the church could *make* the world righteous only through coercion. That would not be a true righteousness rooted in the hope of the eschaton but a false righteousness produced by human effort. It would be the betrayal of hope by the church.

Finally, in the church we learn that we are "on the way"—we have not yet arrived. The disciple community is not our final destination.[22] For this reason the church always witnesses through its life to something beyond itself. The church is not the eschaton, though it is witness to the eschaton. As a people on the way, the church inculcates the virtue of hope by its continual willingness to question its own way of life. Knowing that it is a community created and sustained by God the Holy Spirit, the church has no need to defend or guarantee its own existence.

Being as communal. As the disciple community is formed in the virtue of faith, it fulfills the task of witnessing faithfully to the gospel. In relation to our cultural situation, the church witnesses in several ways.

First, we stand against the individualism of modernity simply by the conviction that we can learn hope only in the disciple community. Community is not formed by the choice of individuals to join together, it is an indispensable characteristic of the eschaton that makes us new beings. The hope in which we live is not a hope for *me* but a hope for *us.*

Second, since the disciple community is a new humanity created by God's transforming power, this creation stands as a witness against the postmodern conviction that we are trapped in our communities and in the differences that mark us. Apart from God's grace, the human condition is marked ineradicably by difference and violence. By God's grace we are made one new humanity living in the peaceableness of hope. This creation of a new humanity also stands as witness against modernity, which attempts to create unity by denying or eradicating difference. In the church we do not "set aside our differences," we bring them as gifts to God and to one another. Our differences are not eradicated but transformed by God's grace into gifts for one another.

As a community on the way, the church witnesses to the eschaton by standing against the modernist project that seeks redemption in the forces of history and human efficacy. We hope for the redemption that comes from God, not from humanity. The church witnesses to the eschaton by rejecting the postmodernist acceptance of violence and difference as "the way things are." As a community on the way, the church is a destabilizing force and disillusioning presence in the world. Since we live in hope, we seek neither to overcome nor to accept the present.

We know that God in Christ comes for the redemptive transformation of this world.

Hope as cosmic. Although we are used to thinking of hope in terms of individual salvation or, at the most, hope for the salvation of all humanity, in the gospel hope is oriented toward the redemption of all creation.[23] As we have already seen, Paul's letter to the Colossians proclaims that "through [Christ] God was pleased to reconcile to himself all things, whether on earth or in heaven" (1:20).[24] This eschatological redemption is proclaimed in the book of Revelation, where John sees "a new heaven and a new earth. . . . And the one who was seated on the throne said, 'See, I am making all things new'" (21:1, 5).

But the clearest expression of the virtue of hope as cosmic is found in Paul's letter to the Romans:

> For the creation waits with eager longing for the revealing of the children of God; for the creation was subjected to futility, not of its own will but by the will of the one who subjected it, in hope that the creation itself will be set free from its bondage to decay and will obtain the freedom of the glory of the children of God. We know that the whole creation has been groaning in labor pains until now; and not only the creation, but we ourselves, who have the first fruits of the Spirit, groan inwardly while we wait for adoption, the redemption of our bodies. For in hope we were saved. Now hope that is seen is not hope. For who hopes for what is seen? But if we hope for what we do not see, we wait for it with patience. (8:19-25)

In this passage Paul clearly ties the hope in which we live to the eschaton of all creation, not just of humanity.

So the virtue of hope habituates our relationship to the whole cosmos. Not only humanity but also the whole creation is made new in Jesus Christ.[25] Now we know the meaning and the future of "all things." Although in the present they may be in rebellion against God, through Christ they have been reconciled. This includes whatever "invisible" forces are at work on us, such as race, class, national identity, economic status, sex and the demonic. Whether we think of these things as social constructs or invisible powers, they participate through the hope of the church in God's redemption.

This does not mean that they are good in themselves; it does mean that they are eschatologically redeemed. In the disciple community that is habituated in hope, the power of these elements of the cosmos over us is exposed as illusory. These elements are real, but they have been redeemed in Jesus Christ. Since we live toward them in hope, we recognize that we must endure their presence with patience, longing for the day when redemption is complete.

In hope as cosmic the disciple community also finds guidance for our relationship to "the visible creation"—to earth and all that is in it. To respond to creation in hope does not mean that we cease to care for it because, after all, God is going to make a new earth. Rather, just as we care for persons outside Christ in hope that they will become part of the new humanity in Christ, so also we care for this creation in hope that it will be part of the new creation.

In the midst of an ecological crisis, the disciple community responds in hope, not in fear. Creation is not an enemy to be defeated or a servant to be ruled.[26] Rather, in hope we see creation as a participant with us in God's redemption. Yet since we wait in hope for the completion of redemption, we also know that what we long for comes only by the gift of God.[27]

In the church today we often seem to be caught between two extremes. On the one hand are those who want to care for this earth because it is the only world we have, and if we do not take care of it, life will come to an end. On the other hand are those who see no need to care for the earth because God is going to make a new one. But if we understand that our hope is cosmic, that the redemption in which we participate is the redemption of all creation, then we will refuse to choose between these alternatives. In contrast to these extremes we will care for this earth because God loved it enough to send his Son to redeem it. We will care for it in hope, not in despair.[28]

Being as cosmic. In the virtue of hope as cosmic we learn that there is nothing in all creation that can threaten our new being in Christ. In him all things that we typically see as threats have been reconciled to God. In our cultural situation this mark of hope profoundly transforms our way of being.

Modernity corrupts creation as "nature," something outside humanity that we master and manipulate. Or it is seen as an enemy that we defeat. For we Christians to live in hope toward creation does not deny that in the present there are forces in the world that threaten human life. At the same time, however, we must also recognize that we humans are the source of the greatest threat. Most important, we know that we are creatures, not gods—we are part of the created order. To live in hope toward creation denies that creation threatens human being.

The work of God that establishes and guarantees our being is the redemption of creation.[29] Since the work of redemption is not complete, we and the rest of the created order groan together as we await the completion. As the disciple community lives in hope, we recognize that the rest of the created order is as much our victim as we are its victim. Our only hope is the reconciliation of all things in Christ.

Postmodernity views the various social constructions of our identity as ineradicable cosmic forces that differentiate us and divide us. For postmodernity, these differences and divisions make violence an inescapable characteristic of humanity. In hope as cosmic the disciple community acknowledges these constructions and exposes their claims to have power over us as an illusion. Through hope as cosmic the disciple community proclaims that these constructions are redeemed in Christ. Such redemption involves judgment, but it is a judgment that works salvation, not condemnation. That knowledge enables us to live toward all creation in hope.

Conclusion

If we return now to the questions raised by the advertisement for *Hope* magazine, how does the Christian virtue of hope respond? In place of hope in "the human spirit" and "the power of human intervention," the gospel habituates in us hope in the coming of God, who redeems the world in Jesus Christ. In response to those who greet human hope with cynicism, the gospel calls us to eschatological hope that marks our way of life even now.

Through the virtue of hope the disciple community is habituated in the way of living between the time of Christ's first coming and his second coming. Formed in the virtue of hope, the disciple community lives eschatologically. Grounded eschatologically, the virtue of hope frees the church from self-concern and self-protection in order that it may witness to the gospel and serve in the name of Jesus Christ. Through this witness and service, the fear of nonbeing and of the future is overcome by something greater than humanity. In hope the cosmos is transformed. This transformation turns differences and divisions that seem to lead inevitably to violence into sources of peace. In a culture marked by fear, anxiety and violence, this gospel-shaped hope is, indeed, the only hope.[30]

Six

SUSTAINING HOPE

The Practice of Worship

• • • • • • • • • • • • • • • • • • • •

Worship is the most significant practice of hope in the midst of our cultural situation. Many of us who gather for worship, however, have not been grasped by this. We view worship as an insignificant addition to the real world. Eugene Peterson comments on this mistake:

> As a pastor, I don't like being viewed as nice but insignificant. I bristle when a high-energy executive leaves the place of worship with the comment, "This was wonderful, Pastor, but now we have to get back to the real world, don't we?" I had thought we were in the most-real world, the world revealed as God's, a world believed to be invaded by God's grace and turning on the pivot of Christ's crucifixion and resurrection. The executive's comment brings me up short; he isn't taking this seriously. Worshiping God is marginal to making money. Prayer is marginal to the bottom line. Christian salvation is a brand preference.[1]

In a world captive to many illusory hopes, even our worship can be distorted to serve those hopes rather than the hope of the gospel. If we are to be habituated in the virtue of hope, we must recover a practice of worship that is sustained by, and sustains, the hope of the gospel.

In this chapter, therefore, I will argue for the recovery of hopeful worship in the midst of modernity and postmodernity. I will begin by considering the relationship between the practice of worship and the church as the institution that sustains worship. This will provide a foundation for examining various ways that our practice of worship and the virtue of hope may be corrupted by our cultural situation. After noting these threats to and opportunities for faithful witness to the gospel in our practice of worship, I will turn to an account of the practice of worship that sustains the virtue of hope.

Worship and the Church

Chapter four considered Alasdair MacIntyre's outline of the characteristics of a practice. This chapter will further develop our understanding of practices by considering the relationship between practices and institutions. As MacIntyre has shown, practices and virtues are intimately related to the institutions that sustain them.[2] Three characteristics of this relationship are pertinent to our concerns.

First, MacIntyre argues that practices and institutions need one another for their sustenance. On the one hand, practices cannot survive for long without being sustained by institutions. On the other hand, institutions are formed by practices. Indeed, the formation of an institution is itself a practice.

Second, however, institutions threaten the integrity of practices. As noted briefly in chapter four, a practice is concerned with "internal goods." In other words, a practice is concerned with goods embodied in the practice itself, not with goods beyond the practice. So, for example, *as a practice,* basketball is played to achieve goods such as teamwork, athletic excellence and the thrill of competition. These are goods achieved only by the actual practice of basketball. As something other than a practice, basketball is played to achieve fame, wealth and glory. These are goods external to the actual practice of basketball.

For us to be engaged in an activity *as a practice,* we must be concerned with achieving goods internal to a practice. In contrast to practices "institutions are typically and characteristically concerned with . . . external goods."[3] Herein lies the conflict between institutions and practices: practices have integrity through their pursuit of internal goods; institutions characteristically seek external goods in order to sustain their existence.

Third, MacIntyre suggests that the virtues are what enables practices "to resist the corrupting power of institutions."[4] For this to happen we need a clear account of the virtues that are appropriate to our conception of the *telos* or, in the case of the church, the eschaton.[5] Then we have to judge the faithfulness of our practices by these virtues. More important, in order to resist the corrupting power of institutions, we must have people, formed by the appropriate virtues, who are shaping our institutions. Having the right rules is not enough to sustain faithful practice. We must also have good people.

What all this means for worship is that we must first recognize that the practice of worship is set within the church as an institution. The form of the church as an institution may vary among cultures and traditions, but its purpose is always the same: to sustain the practices of faithful Christian witness, among them the practice of worship.[6] However, we must also recognize that the institutional life of the church always threatens to corrupt faithful practices in order to achieve some external good, such as success or status. Our practice of worship, then, is one of the criteria by which we may judge the faithfulness of the church. Moreover, we must always be ready to correct the life of the church for it to be formed by gospel virtues. In the church we must seek a practice of worship that is formed by hope as eschatological, christological, communal and cosmic.

Worship as Corrected Vision

In the tradition of virtue ethics vision plays a central role.[7] Our conception of the *telos* determines, more or less, how we "see" the world, and how we see the world shapes a life of virtue. It shapes what we count as important and directs our energies and desires. As the practice of the virtue of hope, worship shapes, and is shaped by, our vision of the world and extends our ability both to see the world through eyes of hope and to live hopefully within the world.

Yet we live in a cultural situation that constantly teaches us to see the world and our lives through eyes other than eyes of hope. In the practice of worship we learn to see the world as it really is. Eugene Peterson's story neatly captures this characteristic of worship—in worship we are in "the most-real world." Worship is the practice of the church that enacts the reality established and revealed by the gospel of Jesus Christ. In the midst of lives that are continually shaped by other visions of reality, worship corrects our vision and enables us to live in hope in every part of our lives.

A biblical account of worship as "corrected vision" is found in Psalm 73. The psalmist begins by confessing, "My feet had almost stumbled; my steps had nearly slipped. For I was envious of the arrogant; I saw the prosperity of the wicked" (vv. 2-3). He goes on to describe what he saw and then concludes his description:

Such are the wicked;
    always at ease, they increase in riches.
All in vain I have kept my heart clean
    and washed my hands in innocence.
For all day long I have been plagued,
    and am punished every morning. (vv. 12-14)

At this point the psalmist's vision is marked by hopelessness—his way of life is "in vain" (v. 13). He begins his recovery of hope by thinking of his community (v. 15), but his vision is cleared and hope recovered only when he "went into the sanctuary of God" (v. 17).

It is significant that this psalm is ascribed to Asaph, who (according to 1 Chron 16:5) was the chief liturgist (worship leader) when the ark of the covenant was brought to Jerusalem. Asaph, worship leader and psalmist without hope, recovers hope as he thinks of the community to which he belongs and either participates in or recalls worship of God in the sanctuary. In the sanctuary his vision is corrected. There he sees the end of the wicked (vv. 17-20). There he sees himself correctly (vv. 21-28) and in hope confesses to God: "Whom have I in heaven but you? And there is nothing on earth that I desire other than you. My flesh and my heart may fail, but God is the strength of my heart and my portion forever" (vv. 25-26).

Psalm 73 is an example of corrected vision. The virtue of hope is shaped in the practice of worship. In our cultural situation we too need the practice of worship that corrects our vision and shapes the virtue of hope. Without this practice our vision is continually distorted and our life corrupted. At the same time, however, without the virtue of hope as the shape of our worship, the practice of worship may also be corrupted.

Isaiah the prophet denounces just such a corruption of worship. In a long passage the prophet begins by denouncing the rulers of Judah as "rulers of Sodom" and the people of Judah as "people of Gomorrah." (Is 1:10). He goes on to describe how much the Lord God detests their worship.

God's denunciation of their worship through the prophet is instructive. There is no hint here that they are neglecting worship or devaluing worship by bringing substandard sacrifices. Indeed, they seem to be fulfilling regulations for worship and have even increased occasions for worship (1:11-14). Moreover, their worship is enthusiastic—they stretch out their hands and "make many prayers" (v. 15).

Isaiah denounces their worship not because it is substandard
and lacking enthusiasm but because the people who are wor-
shiping are people with bloody hands and corrupt lives. He
declares to them God's command:
  Wash yourselves; make yourselves clean;
  remove the evil of your doings from before my eyes;
  cease to do evil,
  learn to do good;
  seek justice,
  rescue the oppressed,
  defend the orphan,
  plead for the widow. (vv. 16-17)
From this passage and the rest of Isaiah 1, we may surmise that
Judah has become a people whose worship is no longer formed
by internal goods. They no longer seek in worship to be formed
into a people who live by hope. They have become a people
whose lives are their own, to do with as they please. They have
forgotten the past, present and future coming of God. Their
worship has become a corrupt attempt to keep God quiet while
they pursue their own lives, oppressing the poor, the orphan and
the widow.

Like Judah, we today may allow—and often have allowed—
our worship to be corrupted. Much that we call worship is dry
and boring because it is no longer a practice sustained by and
sustaining hope. Much that we call worship is hopeless because
it enables us to live in conformity to the illusions of the world
rather than in conformity to the eschaton of the gospel. We need
to recover the practice of worship in hope so that our vision may
be corrected and our witness faithful. In our cultural situation the
practice of worship is particularly vulnerable to four kinds of
corruption.

First, the hopeful practice of worship may be corrupted into
a kind of *mass therapy session*.[8] Various forms of therapy arise as
expressions of modernity's self-salvation. These therapies work

upon the self in order to change my view of my "self" and enable me to cope better with my life. Although some postmodernists subject therapeutic practices to rigorous critique, others seek to recover a practice of psychotherapy under the conditions of postmodernity. Indeed, as the postmodernist conviction that violence marks our being takes hold of our lives, we may turn with even greater passion to therapeutic practices as a means of coping. In these circumstances both modernity and postmodernity threaten to turn our worship into mass therapy.

Worship becomes a form of mass therapy when we put the self and the needs of the self at the center of worship and when we define those needs in terms of our cultural situation rather than in terms of the eschaton. We must be particularly vigilant here. Philip Rieff argues that therapeutic cultures will be characterized by increasing spirituality.[9] In that quest for a therapeutic spirituality, we in the church may see a growth in numbers, but we must also be very aware of two ways in which therapeutic spirituality may corrupt our practice of worship.

Instead of a practice that forms the virtue of hope and conforms us to God's eschaton, worship may simply become a means of coping with the world as it is. Such worship is not the formation of a new being in Christ, nor is it habituation into a new reality. Such worship does not enact the redemption of the world, it simply enables us to cope with a world that is left unchanged. Furthermore, worship as mass therapy does not form the disciple community as a "Christian counterculture." Instead it encourages greater conformity to the world. The corruption of our worship by therapeutic practices does not teach us to be "poor in spirit" and "to mourn" because we see the distance between God's redemption and the world. Rather, therapeutic worship teaches us to accept the world as it is and gives us coping mechanisms for living in the world as it is. Hopeful worship does change our life in the world, but it does so by forming in us the virtue of hope, which enables us to live in the new reality of the eschaton.

The second way that our cultural situation may corrupt our practice of worship is by turning it into a quest for *entertainment*. Through entertainment such as movies, television and visits to Disney World, our culture seeks to create a heightened experience of everyday reality, what some culture critics call *hyperreality*.[10] These experiences turn reality into something we wish it were but which it never really is. We wish our lives were filled with excitement and with dangers that we always survive, but our lives never are. So we create, in our movies and television shows, heroes who face countless dangers that they always conquer. And at amusement parks we experience the "simulacra" (the pretense) of dangers that we always survive.

Our worship is often corrupted by our desire to be entertained, to have a heightened experience of reality. We want the singing, the drama and the preaching to create an "experience" for us that heightens our experience of reality. But worship is not the enactment of "hyperreality," it is the enactment of God's eschatological redemption by the disciple community. This is not a heightened experience of reality but our participation in another reality. We are not an audience being entertained; we are a disciple community, the new humanity, being formed by the power of the Holy Spirit. There is real drama in worship, but it is the drama of our participation in God's act of redemption, not the heightening of our experience of the world. Our hope lies not in intensifying our worldly lives but in intensifying our participation in the gospel of Jesus Christ, which is the redemption of the world.

In addition to corrupting our worship by turning it into mass therapy or entertainment, our culture may corrupt the practice of worship by turning it into *a political rally*. Through this corruption worship becomes simply a time to rally those who have political responsibilities in the world. This corruption is subtle, because the community of disciples that is formed in worship certainly has a "politics."[11] That is, we in the church have convictions about who we are as human beings, how we are to relate to one another and the good that we should seek through our corporate life. But those are convictions about the new humanity that is being formed by God's act of redemption. They are not convictions about how to organize the world. They are convictions that call the world to conversion not to reorganization.

Understood in this way, the politics of the church is the enactment of an alternative to the world.[12] If this is the church's politics, then the most political act of the church is worship. In worship we enact the political order of the new humanity, and we witness to God's redemption of the world. In our worship God invites the world to be made new, not to be made better. In worship we learn that the hope of the world lies not in the world's power but in God's eschaton.[13]

Worship as Eschatological

For the practice of worship to form and sustain the virtue of hope, it must itself be formed and sustained by the various characteristics of hope—it must be eschatological, christological, communal and cosmic. At the same time, worship as a practice comprises many distinct elements. To develop our account of the practice of worship, I will first consider the relationship between worship and hope as eschatological. Then, rather than considering the practice of worship in relation to the other characteristics of hope, I will consider the various elements of worship and the ways in which they are formed by, and form, the virtue of hope.

Worship is *the* eschatological act of the church.[14] Through worship we participate in the eschaton and enact God's redemption, God's new creation. Through the practice of worship as eschatological we are formed in the virtue of hope that habituates us in the way of being in between the times of Christ's coming.[15]

The apostle John's visions of heaven are filled with acts of worship. In the early chapters of Revelation the saints are gathered around the throne of God, offering praise to God and to the Lamb. They praise God for creation:

You are worthy, our Lord and God,

to receive glory and honor and power,

for you created all things,

   and by your will they existed and were created. (4:11)

The saints praise the Lamb for redemption:

You are worthy to take the scroll

   and to open its seals,

for you were slaughtered and by your blood you ransomed

   for God

   saints from every tribe and language and people and nation;

you have made them to be a kingdom and priests serving our

   God,

   and they will reign on earth. (5:9-10)

In these verses we have an entire description of the virtue of hope embodied in worship. The saints declare that through creation and redemption all being depends on God. Through their declaration that the Lamb is worthy to open the scroll that contains the meaning of history, they confess that he is the meaning of history. Through their recognition that the redeemed are from all tribes, languages, peoples and nations, they acknowledge that in the new humanity our differences have made peace. And they look forward to the time when that new humanity will inherit the earth and reign upon it.

When we worship eschatologically, our worship is joined by the power of God's Spirit with this worship in heaven.[16] Death is overcome. Those who have died in the Lord are not separated from us. We worship with them, and our worship then becomes our act of participation in the eschaton. Understood in this way, the practice of worship is sustained by and sustains the virtue of hope.

We may understand worship as an eschatological act in another way—God dwelling with us. After John sees "a new heaven and a new earth" (Rev 21:1), he tells us that he

> heard a loud voice from the throne saying,
> "See, the home of God is among mortals.
> He will dwell with them as their God;
> they will be his peoples,
> and God himself will be with them;
> he will wipe every tear from their eyes.
> Death will be no more;
> mourning and crying and pain will be no more,
> for the first things have passed away." (21:3-4)

When, through hope, we engage in worship as an eschatological practice, God dwells with us. Through hopeful worship we participate in fellowship with God as an anticipation of the fulfillment of God's redemption of creation.[17]

The eschatological character of worship may also be identified by considering the *time* of worship.[18] For the church, worship is a practice of the sabbath, and keeping the sabbath is an act of hope.[19] When we keep the sabbath by resting from our labors, we acknowledge that our life, our way of being, is sustained by God. We rest from our labors because we know that our hope is in the Lord, not in our labors. Sabbath rest also reflects our larger hope in the Lord for the sustenance of creation and for the completion of redemption. It is in that restful hope that we gather to worship and celebrate God's gift of being. God is worthy of our praise because God, not humanity, creates and redeems.

In our culture and in many Christian communities, sabbath keeping is no longer practiced. We consider sabbath keeping a burden rather than a blessing. This is a sign, first, of the church's captivity to our culture.[20] But it is also a sign of our lack of understanding. The sabbath is a time to turn from the anxieties and violence of the world and to the hope and peaceableness of the eschaton.

If we truly long for the eschaton, we will look in hope toward sabbath worship. If we seek to worship without keeping the sabbath, then we undermine and even deny in the rest of the day what we have celebrated in worship. Such contradictory activity exposes our lack of hope and vitiates the habituation of our lives in hope. In this instance our fears and anxieties that drive us to labor on the sabbath keep us from the gospel virtue that would relieve those fears and anxieties. If in resistance to our culture we commit ourselves to the practice of worship and sabbath keeping, the virtue of hope will begin to form in us a way of being marked by peace. Thus the practice of worship is one of our most powerful witnesses to the hope of the gospel.

I must make one additional point. In the preceding paragraphs I have emphasized worship as an eschatological practice in order to help us recover a hopeful worship. Worship, however, is not the only place in our life where we participate in the eschaton. Since hope is a cosmic virtue, the entire cosmos, including all our life, participates in the eschaton. So we cannot segregate worship as an eschatological practice from the rest of life. Rather, worship is important because that is where we practice the hope of the gospel. In the practice of worship we participate in the redemption that claims the entire cosmos.[21] In the practice of worship we participate in "the most-real world" so that we may by hope live in this most-real world and witness to it in all of life.

The Elements of Worship

Today worship is perhaps more fragmented than ever before. Some church traditions follow a structured, historically grounded, written liturgy or pattern of worship. Others have a structured, historically grounded, but unwritten liturgy. Some follow the same pattern weekly, others vary the pattern. Some congregations seek to set aside structure in order to free the Spirit to guide worship.

We should not let these differences distract us from the central issues regarding the practice of worship. If worship is our response to and participation in God's eschatological work of redemption, then our practice of worship must be guided by the eschaton. Moreover, our practice of worship must correct our vision so that we see through the illusions of reality, hope and hopelessness in our culture. Our pattern of worship is meant to serve these characteristics of worship, not become an end in itself. At the same time, the call to hopeful worship does not legitimize casual, careless or thoughtless approaches to worship. In worship we are engaged with the most-real world and thus in the most serious work to which humans are called.

In the following account, I will describe various elements of worship as they embody the hope that we have in the gospel. I do not mean to commend one worship tradition over another. But I do mean to commend my description of these elements as proper to a practice of worship formed by and forming hope. The various elements of worship enact and extend the virtue of hope.

Invocation. When we begin worship by "invoking" the presence of God or by *epiclesis*—"calling upon" the Holy Spirit—we are not asserting our control over God. Rather, we are confessing that only the coming of God makes us fit for worship. Only by our participation in eschatological redemption may we enter God's presence to worship. Although invocation and *epiclesis* may take many different forms, our worship is formed by hope and sustains hope only if we recognize that we worship not by our own power but by the power of God's Spirit. As Saliers notes, "The Spirit of God who searches all human hearts is the only power able to make us present to God in the midst of our forgetfulness of being."[22] Our worship engages the most-real world not because of our own efforts but because of God's gracious acts.

Confession. As we acknowledge our dependence on God through invocation and *epiclesis,* we are reminded that our hope is in the Lord. This reminder leads us to confession of our own unworthiness and of our many sinful attempts to establish hope on the basis of our own worth and being. Through confession we not only acknowledge our sin, we expose the illusions that lead us astray and cause us to rebel.

If we do not expose these illusions, they become the basis for presumption and idolatry.[23] In the passage from Isaiah 1 that we considered earlier, the presumption and idolatry that had taken hold of Judah could only be remedied by confession of sin and consequent transformation. Our own worship is acceptable and glorifying to God only when it is grounded in confession that comes from hope. Such confession is not easy to practice.

Kefa Sempangi tells the story of one church that came to know the grace of confession. In *A Distant Grief* Sempangi tells the story of his encounter with the East African Revival Fellowship:

> I walked into my first Revival Fellowship meeting shortly after my conversion in 1961. It was Friday afternoon and the hall was packed with people singing and praising God. Most of the songs were about the blood of the Lamb that was slain. As different brethren stood up and openly confessed their sin, I noticed that no one was paying any attention to the sins confessed. Before a brother or sister could finish the confession, the rest of the brethren burst out into songs of praise.[24]

As one of the revival leaders later explained to Sempangi, God's grace and the power of the resurrection sustain the healing practice of confession.[25] This practice of confession and knowledge of God's power helped sustain the faithful witness of the Redeemed Church of Uganda during the demonic atrocities that marked the rule of Idi Amin.

In the midst of this fallen world and our own sin, we worship in hope of God's eschatological redemption as we willingly confess our sins to God. This confession enacts the most-real world that will sustain our witness in the midst of the obvious evil of Idi Amin and in the midst of the more subtle evils of our own culture.

Forgiveness. In worship the disciple community not only confesses sin, it also receives and enacts the forgiveness that is ours in hope. Confession arises as we realize our unworthiness before God. We are enabled to confess our sin rather than deny it because of the hope of forgiveness that we have in the gospel. When we confess our sin in worship, we acknowledge that sin is not a private affair. Rather, sin is the root of our divisions and our violence. Through the forgiveness of sin, we are set free from that violence and united in peaceableness.[26]

This forgiveness is not merely a setting free. It is also a transformation of our lives in hope. In hope we are made a new humanity, a holy people with "an ability to stop the cycles of sin and violence without passing them on to others."[27] Through the forgiveness of sin enacted in worship, we are habituated in a hope marked by the peaceableness of the eschaton in which God redeems our lives and all creation.

Praise and thanksgiving. In the practice of worship sustained by hope, praise and thanksgiving are not the manipulation of God into giving us more or ignoring our sin. Rather, the praise and thanksgiving of hopeful worship is a celebration of the eschaton in which God has already given us all things. Directing our praise and thanksgiving to God corrects our vision and transforms our tendency to ascribe the good things of life to our own powers. In worship we are trained to see the goodness of life as God's gifts in creation and redemption.

At the same time, praise and thanksgiving transform our "natural" desires. In Psalm 73:3-12 the psalmist begins by desiring the possessions of the wicked—wealth, ease, acclamation. But through worship this desire is transformed: "Whom have I in heaven but you? And there is nothing on earth I desire other than you" (v. 25). In worship we are trained to look in hope to the eschaton of God as the source of our being and the fulfillment of our desires.

When we enter into worship on a Sunday morning, I suspect

that many of us are like the psalmist. We come from a week of
activities that have shaped our desires. We come wanting greater
confidence at work or at home, desiring the newest product that
advertisers have placed before us, feeling inadequate in every
way and wanting those inadequacies overcome in ways that the
world offers. In other words, we come with an attitude of praise
for things that will make us more adequate in the world. Wendell
Berry captures this attitude in his poem "Manifesto: The Mad
Farmer Liberation Front":

> Love the quick profit, the annual raise,
> vacation with pay. Want more
> of everything ready-made. Be afraid
> to know your neighbors and to die.
> And you will have a window in your head.
> Not even your future will be a mystery
> any more. Your mind will be punched in a card
> and shut away in a little drawer.
> When they want you to buy something
> they will call you. When they want you
> to die for profit they will let you know.[28]

What we learn in worship is that God has already given us
everything in Jesus Christ. As we see the world and our lives in
the world in light of God's work of redemption, we are made fit
for the kingdom of God—and misfit for the world. As we praise
God for those gifts, we discipline and redirect our desires. As we
engage the eschaton in our worship, we learn, in the concluding
words of Berry's poem, to "practice resurrection."[29]

Lament and intercession. In one sense all of worship, indeed
all of life, is prayer. But our practice of worship also contains
specific forms of prayer that are sustained by hope.

In lament we acknowledge before God the distance between
this world and the eschaton. In the same breath that we praise
God for the goodness of life, we also must acknowledge the
suffering and violence that marks life. In lament we bring the

suffering of the world before God. When we do this, lament is an expression of hope, not despair. By bringing suffering before God in lament, we acknowledge that God is the only hope of redeeming suffering. By this acknowledgment hope habituates us in a way of being that is rooted in the eschaton rather than in our own human powers, which apart from the gospel simply add to the violence and suffering of the world. Through lament we embody the hope that God in Christ comes to redeem a suffering world.

To lament we add intercession. Through intercession we acknowledge that the world is not yet fully redeemed and, at the same time, enact the conviction of hope that God is even now at work in the world by the power of the Holy Spirit. Through intercession we pray in particular ways for the coming of God. Through intercession we pray for his coming in our own lives, in the lives of those around us and, indeed, for the whole world. Through intercession we embody the hope that is communal and cosmic.

Offering. In the offering of the fruit of our labors—for most of us, our money—we enact our hope in God by resisting our culture. In a culture that has a deeply distorted view of money and worth and that often measures being in terms of money, to give away our money is profound training in hope. In hope we offer our money to God in order to confess and expose our captivity to an idol. In hope we offer our money to God in recognition that all our gifts come from God and that only God sustains our being.

Here we must be vigilant against the corrupting power of an institutional view of the church. Even the church as the disciple community is sustained by hope, not by money. We do not offer our money to sustain the church, for the church is sustained in hope, which is enacted by our offerings. We do not offer our money in payment for services rendered to us by God or the church. God has given us the very life and energy that enables us to labor, so our offerings simply give back to God what belongs already to God. Our offerings are an act of hope that further habituates us in the conviction that in the most-real world our being is a gift from God.

Proclamation. Although our entire practice of worship is a proclamation of the hope of the gospel, we proclaim the gospel in particular ways through Bible reading, testimony and preaching. Through these acts we acknowledge that redemption has come through Jesus Christ but is not yet complete in us or the world. As a result of this incompleteness we need continually to be reminded of the source and goal of our hope, continual witness to the work of redemption in our world today, continual instruction in the way of being that is rooted in the gospel and continual discernment both of the illusions of hope that so often captivate us and of the distance between the world and the eschaton. Through proclamation the most-real world of the gospel is set before us so that we sustain and are sustained by the hope of the gospel.

Commitment. In all the elements of worship we sustain and are sustained by the virtue of hope through the power of the Holy Spirit. This hope is not confined to our formal worship as a disciple community, for hope is for the entire world. We cannot, therefore, leave hope behind when we leave worship. If we are truly formed in hope by the practice of worship, we take that hope wherever we go. So worship also involves the commitment and recommitment of our whole life to the gospel of hope.

Although worship is integral to the mission of the church—and is itself part of the mission of the church—worship also corrects our vision and transforms us into a new humanity that can live and witness more faithfully in the world. Therefore in our worship we are trained in and commit ourselves to our mission in the world as the disciple community.[30]

Baptism, Communion, footwashing. Three other acts of worship sustain and are sustained by the virtue of hope.[31]

First, baptism celebrates the new humanity created by God. As Saliers notes, "The witness of baptism is a present way of life, the new creature is appearing. The church as the baptismal and baptizing community is itself to be a sign, a living witness to the hope."[32] In baptism we celebrate the eschaton that is God's redemption. We acknowledge that our "old" being is marked by sin and violence and needs to be killed in order to put an end to that sin and violence.[33] We enact the new being that we have as a gift from God. Thus in baptism we sustain and are sustained by our only hope of redemption. Further, baptism not only enacts our new being in Christ, it also represents our habituation into that new being as we "live into our baptism."[34]

In the Eucharist we celebrate a meal that recalls Jesus' life, death and resurrection, that declares his presence as our host at the table and that looks forward to the future banquet that we will share with him. The tensions between this past, present and future habituate us in the hope that marks our new being. Remembering his past, we learn that our being is sustained by his sacrifice. Discerning his presence, we learn that we are transformed by his power. Looking to his future, we learn that the world will one day be fully redeemed. In all of this we are incorporated into the story of Christ's life—God's work of redemption—so that the virtue of hope may form us into the life of the new humanity.[35]

Finally, although few Christian traditions today consider the act of footwashing on a par with baptism and the Eucharist, some do treat it as equal, and many that do not regard it as equal nevertheless practice it in some form. Since footwashing is so little practiced and so seldom examined, it really deserves more extensive discussion than I can give it here. What I do want to note is the enactment through footwashing of an absence of self-regard. In this there is a powerful declaration that our being is not something that we must protect and preserve. Rather, in footwashing we give ourselves away in service to others.

I learned something of this in the Free Will Baptist tradition in which I was raised. Free Will Baptists are among the minority of churches that regularly practice footwashing. When I attended one footwashing service as an adolescent and very uncertain of my relationship to Jesus Christ, a professor of theology from the denominational college approached me and asked if he could wash my feet. I still remember my initial feelings of unworthiness and my subsequent feelings of great worth as Leroy Forlines knelt to wash my feet. Someone of great status had lifted me up through his act of humility and disregard for self.

In Jesus' act of footwashing we see encapsulated his entire attitude of service, his laying aside of himself and his lifting us up to God. When we earlier considered this act of footwashing, we saw how clearly it was rooted in Jesus' hope—he knew "that he had come from God and was going to God" (Jn 13:3).[36] It is no less so for us: in footwashing we embody the virtue of hope that knows that the source and goal of our being is guaranteed by God in Christ. So in our hope of the eschaton we can become one another's servants in this act and in our whole life.

Conclusion

In these various elements we have an account of the practice of worship that is sustained by and sustains the virtue of hope. We are habituated in the *eschatological* character of hopeful worship by the time of our worship and by our participation in God's redemption. We are habituated in the *personal* character of hopeful worship by our recognition that we are worthy to worship only through the person of Jesus Christ and by our personal transformation through the practice of worship. We are habituated in the *communal* character of hopeful worship by the formation of the new humanity and by our participation in worship with the saints in heaven. We are habituated in the *cosmic* character of worship by the use of our bodies to worship God, by the incorporation of all creation in our worship—praise and thanksgiving for the goodness of creation, lament and intercession for the brokenness of creation, offering the fruit of our labors, the water of baptism (and footwashing), the wine and bread of Communion—and by our commitment to mission in the world.

In the midst of a world marked by violence, false hope and hopelessness, faithful witness to the gospel requires that we live by the hope of the eschaton. Such witness begins and ends in worship. Our lives are so corrupted by the world that the only possibility of hopeful worship lies in the power of the risen Lord through the presence of the Holy Spirit. Since he is the One who sustains our very being, we can look with confidence to him as our only hope.

Seven

LOVE AND THE CHRISTIAN WAY OF DOING

· ·

IN THIS CHAPTER I WILL CONCLUDE OUR CONSIDERATION OF the theological virtues with an account of the virtue of love. Any attempt to give a meaningful account of love faces many difficulties. In our culture the word is overused and sentimentalized. In the theological tradition the literature is vast and the issues complex. In popular usage the meaning of love has become so elastic that it has little significance. Today we use the same word to describe our relationship to the brand of shampoo we use, the kind of car we drive and the God we worship. And we have great difficulty differentiating among these loves.

In the theological tradition we have wrestled with many complex issues regarding love and have produced an enormous body of literature. Do the different Greek words for love signify different kinds of love?[1] Do they compete with each other, complement each other or have some other relationship?[2] Is love the one inviolable "rule" of the Christian life?[3]

Moreover, when we seek not merely to talk about love but

also to *act* in love, our cultural situation presents numerous obstacles. Modernity's culture of consumption has turned love into another commodity for exchange. I give love in return for something, or I receive something that then obligates me to love. Postmodernity, on the other hand, denies the possibility of love. If the will to power ineradicably marks the human condition, then love is simply power disguised. When I say that I love you, I am exercising some kind of power over you. In this instance postmodernity accepts with cynical realism the result of modernity turning love into a medium of exchange—love is simply one language by which we negotiate power.

In spite of these difficulties we cannot abandon the language of love in our witness to the gospel. Love is at the very heart of the New Testament accounts of redemption in Jesus Christ. To abandon love would be to cut the heart out of the gospel. Rather than abandon love, we need to recover a gospel-shaped life of love. Instead of allowing our practices and our culture to determine what love means and then attempting to fit the gospel into that understanding of love, we need to allow the gospel to determine how we speak of love.

If it were possible, the disciple community could make progress in our understanding by declaring a five-year ban on the use of the word *love*. During that time we would concentrate on living according to the gospel. After five years the ban would be lifted and we could begin to speak of love in fresh and illuminating ways. But how could it be possible? How could we live or speak of the gospel without the language of love?

Since it is not possible for us to live according to the gospel without the language of love, I propose another means of recovering a gospel-shaped love—by thinking of love as a virtue. I will examine the many difficulties that distort our understanding and practice of love. In this account *love* is not an empty term that we can fill with whatever meaning we want. Love is one way of describing the life of the disciple community as it is transformed by the power of the Holy Spirit in faithfulness to the gospel.

So as I consider love as a virtue I will examine some of the questions about love that have been raised by the tradition in order to deepen our understanding of what it means to think of love as a virtue. I will correct some misconceptions of love and focus on habituation as a mark of the virtue of love. Also, I will identify several aspects of our cultural situation that represent dangers and opportunities for the faithful witness of the church through habituation in love. Then I will develop an account of the virtue of love which is evangelical, spiritual, natural and communal.

Although *evangelical* is a term used to describe a particular tradition and community within Christianity, I will use it to refer more broadly to the gospel. To describe the virtue of love as evangelical is to assert that the gospel of Jesus Christ reveals the true character of love. When I consider love as spiritual, I will not be contrasting spiritual love with physical love but considering how the Spirit of Jesus Christ transforms all love.

Then I will consider how this work of the Spirit enables us to love "naturally." The claim that love is natural may initially seem odd in that it contradicts the claim that love is the work of the Spirit. But love, rather than being a denial of our humanity, is the fulfillment of our humanity.

When we consider love as communal, I will argue that love overcomes our divisions and our violence through the redemptive work of Christ. In all this, love is a mark of the being of the new humanity that transforms our way of doing. What we need are not more *words* of love but more *acts* of love that witness to the gospel and give depth and meaning to our words.

Love as a Virtue in the Theological Tradition

To consider love as a virtue is to consider love as a character trait of disciples of Jesus Christ. As a trait of Christian character, love is not something that a person can set aside whenever he or she chooses to do so. Rather, to have love as a virtue is to be so habituated in love that a person's whole being and doing is transformed by a love that is inescapable. This inescapable love may be understood better by considering some of the questions raised by the theological tradition.

One of those questions is the possibility of conflict between the four forms of love. Some distinguish between the natural affection that we have for persons such as family members, the deeper nature of friendship, the strong attraction of eros and the self-giving of charity.[4] The differences between these forms of love may induce us to think of them as rivals.[5] For example, if friendship teaches us to prefer our friends over others, doesn't this preference work against charity, which teaches us to love everyone the same?

The apparent rivalry between the various loves may be resolved when we think of love as a virtue.[6] As such, we consider love as a habit of the Christian life that marks all our relationships, all our being and doing. Thus the virtue of love teaches us the appropriate way of acting in all our relationships.[7] Love takes many different forms, but all those forms are given unity by the character of the person acting in love.

Of course, since no one's love is perfect in this life, individuals will face many conflicts. But those conflicts are not a sign of rivalry among the forms of love but a sign of human incompleteness. These conflicts are not resolved by weighing the claims of various loves and deciding which has the greater claim. They are resolved by growing in love—becoming more habituated in the virtue of love—so that a person may act in ways appropriate to the gospel in particular situations.[8]

If we understand love as a virtue formed by the eschaton of the gospel, then love is given a particular shape and direction that is determined by the gospel, not by the "objects" of love. The disciple who is formed in love, therefore, discerns how God is at work in the world and responds to the particular dimensions of a situation in the light of that discernment. That response may be given the name *affection, friendship, eros* or *charity,* but if it is determined by the gospel, it is an act of love.

Another question raised by theological tradition concerns the relationship between love and other virtues. For Thomas Aquinas, this relationship depends on the question we are asking. If we are asking where virtue begins (what he calls "the order of generation"), then faith precedes hope and love because faith is the means by which we come to know that which "we hope for and love." But if we are asking where virtue is headed (what he calls "the order of perfection"), then "charity precedes faith and hope in that both faith and hope are formed by charity and so acquire the perfection of virtue. Charity is thus the mother and root of all virtues insofar as it is the form of all virtues."[9] With this assertion Thomas simply reflects the claims of Paul: "And now faith, hope, and love abide, these three; and the greatest of these is love" (1 Cor 13:13). Even more clearly in relation to our question about relationships among the virtues, Paul, after listing such virtues as compassion, kindness, humility, meekness and patience (Col 3:12-13), says, "Above all, clothe yourselves with love, which binds everything together in perfect harmony" (v. 14).

These statements teach that love as a virtue is the heart of faithful witness to the gospel. Love is not whatever we make it, however. Love is what the gospel makes us. Love is not a description that we are free to attach to whatever we feel most deeply about. Love is the description of a life that has been transformed by the gospel of Jesus Christ. For this reason, we in the disciple community should be more careful in our use of the word *love* so that we may be habituated into the gospel in all that we do.

Why We Need Love as a Virtue
To begin to be faithful to the gospel by bringing all that we do

under the rule of the virtue of love, we must correct a number of misunderstandings and prepare to meet the challenges of our cultural situation. First, we must understand that love is more than a special way of feeling. Indeed, it may be best to say that love is *not* a special way of feeling. In our culture generally and in the church particularly, we often—perhaps usually—use love to refer to a feeling.[10] But feelings follow our moods and are transient in nature. Love that is rooted in the gospel is not something that depends on my mood, nor is it a temporary mark of the Christian. Though moods and changes are true of us at times, we know that the gospel describes love in much stronger terms. In the gospel, love is a settled way of acting toward God and our neighbor. It is a virtue.

The language of virtue reminds us of this characteristic of gospel-love and helps us identify its formation in the disciple community. The love to which we are called by the gospel is to be a habitual mark of the disciple, not a transient feeling that depends on my mood. This love requires training and practice in order for us to be formed in it. It requires the presence of a community that will guide and correct us as we learn love. In other words, this love is a virtue that guides the Christian way of doing.

Second, we must also correct our notion that love is merely obedience to a divine command. As we saw in chapter two, the notion that the Christian life is one of obedience to divine commands is powerful. Certainly Jesus Christ commanded many things, and chief among them is that those who follow him must love. But to reduce love to obedience to divine command is to miss the importance of who is commanding love, who is able to obey and the purpose of that obedience.

When we reduce love to obedience, we obscure the character of the God who commands us to love. That God is not just any god, who could command any action and by that command make any action good. Rather, the God who commands love is the God who comes in Jesus Christ to give his life for the redemption of the world. So the command to love is the command to love in the way that is revealed in Jesus' life, death and resurrection.[11]

When we reduce love to obedience, we also obscure the importance of character in those who obey. Love is not an occasional act of disciples that can be called up at will. Rather, love is the disciples' way of life. Certainly it begins with our decisions, enabled by the Holy Spirit, to act in love. But through the power of the Holy Spirit disciples are transformed by their obedience into those who love because it is their character to do so, not because they consider the various options and decide to love.

When we reduce love to obedience, we mistake the purpose of our obedience to Christ. The purpose of obedience is to form us into mature disciples of Jesus Christ. We are not disciples of a set of rules or of a law, we are disciples of a person, Jesus Christ. Obedience may begin in submission to authority, but obedience to Jesus Christ has the purpose ultimately of transforming us into those who love as God loves in Christ. That is, we are to grow into a love that is not obedience to external law but an act of our very being.

The third error we must correct is the notion that love is a principle or rule that we follow or, even more erroneous, that it is the only principle or rule of the Christian life.[12]

These claims make several errors that may be corrected by thinking of love as a virtue. Virtue turns our attention to important aspects of faithful living that are obscured by an emphasis on principle or rule. Virtue reminds us that we must attend to the formation of disciples in the gospel of Jesus Christ. This formation is crucial to our ability to discern our situation and act in faithfulness to the gospel. An emphasis on principles or rules tends to neglect the importance of formation by acting as if the "loving thing to do" may be perceived without habituation in the virtue of love. Furthermore, virtue turns our attention to God's continuing work of redemption that habituates us in love. To reduce that work to a principle or a rule is to neglect the continuing reality of God's work. Principles and rules do not identify that reality; disciples who are formed in love discern that reality.

To say that love is the perfection of the virtues is to say that love is not all we need. To say that love is the form of the virtues is to say that we need the other virtues. These other virtues are not canceled by love, they are perfected and united by love. This assertion teaches us the proper role of love, but it does not set aside the necessity of growing in other virtues as well. To say that love is the greatest virtue is not to say that love is the only virtue.

Thus love as a virtue is the habituation of us disciples in the gospel of Jesus Christ that enables us to act in faithfulness to that good news. Laws and rules cannot cover every conceivable challenge that we face as disciples. In the New Testament the continuing guidance of the Spirit is described more in terms of virtues, fruit and character than in terms of command. Mature disciples are those who act according to the gospel because they have been formed in the virtue of love.

Modern and Postmodern Threats to Love

Our cultural situation presents many threats to gospel faithfulness that we can meet only if we are formed in the virtue of love. Modernity poses two threats to the virtue of love.

First, modernity enshrines the freedom of the individual from all tyranny, whether that tyranny be political, religious or the claims of another. The individual is bound only by the claims that are self-chosen. The love of the gospel stands over against this kind of freedom. Yes, the gospel sets us free, but that freedom is the freedom to love. If love is acting toward others in ways appropriate to the eschaton, then the freedom of love binds us even more closely. As Paul wrote, "You were called to freedom, brothers and sisters; only do not use your freedom as an opportunity for self-indulgence, but through love become slaves to one another" (Gal 5:13).

Since there is such a conflict between the freedom of modernity and the freedom of the gospel, modernity threatens to corrupt our love into something that appears to act for the other but instead is simply a covert act of self-seeking and self-indulgence. Therefore we have to discern how to act in love without it being a clever act of self-assertion.

The second threat presented by modernity is its drive to turn everything, including love, into a medium of exchange. Thus I "love" my children in order to get from them the behavior that I want, and I "love" my spouse in order to get the kind of relationship that I want. If my children behave badly or my spouse responds unacceptably, then I have struck a "bad bargain" and I no longer "owe" them my love. I am then free to sever the relationships because they have broken our "contract."

In the church we have been corrupted by this way of thinking when we "commodify" our relationship to God and to one another. We may begin to think that God loves us in order to get from us the kind of behavior that he wants from us. Or we may begin to think that our love for God gives us claims on him, that it builds up "divine credit" on which we may draw.

This way of thinking about love corrupts the gospel of Jesus Christ that forms us in love. Love is not a medium of exchange. In Jesus Christ, God loves us unconditionally and is at work redeeming the world from the violence and death brought by sin. Love is not a reward that God offers to us as something we can have if we will be redeemed. Rather, God's love *is* God's redemption. When we participate in that redemption, we are "rescued . . . from the power of darkness and transferred . . . into the kingdom of [God's] beloved Son, in whom we have redemption, the forgiveness of sins" (Col 1:13-14). Our love does not purchase our redemption—it does not buy us anything. We have, through Christ, already been given all that we need. Our love is simply this new life that we have been given.

In postmodernity the virtue of love is threatened by the cynical conviction that all acts are covert expressions of "the will to power." Love is simply the approved way of gaining power in the disciple community. This postmodern critique, for all its cynicism, may help us discern ways in which we practice love as a means of gaining power over God or others. But we must not succumb to the cynicism of postmodernity that considers the will to power inescapable.

In our account of the virtue of love as formed by the gospel, we must show how love is not a quest for power. We must show how the new being, created by the power of the Holy Spirit, acts in love without seeking power. Furthermore, we must show how the gospel reveals that love, not violence, is the true mark of the human condition.

In the end, of course, what we need is not a better account of love but a disciple community that is habituated in the gospel virtue of love. Only that community can witness faithfully to the gospel in the midst of a culture that views others as a means of self-assertion or self-realization. Only a disciple community acting in love can witness faithfully in the midst of a culture marked by the nihilism of power and violence. We live in a world that desperately needs the good news of Jesus Christ embodied in a people that are being formed in the virtue of love.

Love and the Christian Way of Doing

I have identified several challenges faced by the disciple community as we seek to be formed in the virtue of love as a guide to the Christian way of doing. Along the way I have indicated how the virtue of love may help the community meet those challenges. Now I will develop an account of the virtue of love as evangelical, spiritual, natural and communal.

Love as evangelical. As I noted earlier, by *evangelical* I am not ascribing the virtue of love to a particular group within the church. Rather, I mean to identify the virtue of love as "gospel-shaped." Since *love* can be easily twisted in many ways, the gospel of Jesus Christ must be determinative for the disciple community that seeks to witness faithfully through the virtue of love.

To put it in the words of Alasdair MacIntyre, the gospel is "the living tradition" within which our Christian lives are embedded. To say, however, that the gospel is the living tradition of the church is to transform the concept of a living tradition.[13] The gospel is better identified as "the everlasting reality of God's redemption" than as simply "a living tradition" because the former captures the priority of God's work and begins to specify the nature of the gospel. This everlasting reality of God's redemption is what gives the virtue of love its ground and its goal.

The virtue of love that is evangelical will first of all be directed toward action. Although love involves deep affection, that deep affection is revealed only by what we do. In Jesus Christ, God *acts* in love to redeem the world. In a passage that has almost lost its power through overuse, the gospel of John proclaims, "For God so loved the world that he gave his only Son, so that everyone who believes in him may not perish but may have eternal life" (Jn 3:16). When John later affirms that "God is love" (1 Jn 4:8), that assertion is simply a shorthand description of God's action: "God's love was revealed among us in this way: God sent his only Son into the world so that we might live through him" (4:9).[14]

Thus the evangelical virtue of love must be embodied in action. Words, concepts and ideas may guide us, remind us, admonish us and correct us, but witness to the gospel is ultimately the witness of the life of the disciple community. When the life of the disciple community witnesses faithfully to the gospel, then words may also follow as a way of identifying, for an inquiring world, the reason for our way of life.[15] When the life of the disciple community is unfaithful, words become a means of correcting our life and witnessing to the good news that God remains faithful by forgiving our sin and restoring our life. But even here the goal is the restoration of the life of faithfulness to doing the truth. The truth of the gospel is something we are called to do, and the virtue of love guides us in that task.

When by the virtue of love our doing is faithful to the gospel, then it is also sacrificial. More than that, it is *self*-sacrificial. The act of self-sacrifice is, of course, at the heart of the gospel. In Jesus Christ, God gave himself for the sin of the world to redeem the world. We are often tempted to offer a theory in support of this proclamation, but here I will follow a different path. Rather than trying to propose a theory that supports the proclamation, I will identify the implications of the statement that Christ's sacrifice is our redemption.

When by the Holy Spirit we participate in this redemption and know it to be true, we must acknowledge several things, which may serve as guides for the disciple community in the Christian way of doing. First, when we believe that the sacrifice of Christ redeems the world, we must also believe that the peace of God is stronger than the violence of the world. Certainly the crucifixion displays the violence of the world. But in Jesus' willing sacrifice the cross also reveals the power of God's peace. Second, we must believe that God's love is stronger than death.[16] At the heart of creation is not the nonbeing of death but the being of life revealed in Jesus Christ.[17] Third, we must believe that we find our life through the gift of God in Jesus Christ.

If the virtue of love is shaped by this gospel, it will be marked by self-giving. This self-giving bears witness to the gospel of peace not by denying the violence of the world but by embodying "a new world, a *world without deception and injustice*."[18] This self-giving of the virtue of love also bears witness to the gospel of life not by denying death but by embodying eternal life, a life beyond death. In a world marked by violence and death, self-giving is not a quixotic denial of the world, it is life in the new world established by Christ's sacrifice. Only by acting in love formed by this gospel does the disciple community bear faithful witness to Jesus Christ.

Love that is evangelical is not only active and self-giving, it is also responsive. By *responsive* I mean that the virtue of love grows out of our response to God's love for us and responds to others according to the gospel of Jesus Christ.[19] In one sense then, evangelical love is universal because it is shaped by the gospel that enacts God's love for the world. In another sense, evangelical love is particular because it responds to others according to the eschaton of the gospel.

We can see this at work in the life of Jesus. Since he is God, he is love, and his love is directed toward all persons. Yet he responds with love in different ways to different people. In Luke 6:20-26, for example, he pronounces both blessings and woes. The pronouncement of blessing is an act of evangelical love toward those who are poor, hungry, weeping and hated. The pronouncement of woe is an act of evangelical love toward those who are rich, full, laughing and well-spoken of.

Today this evangelical love is embodied in the life of people such as John Perkins.[20] Perkins is an African-American man who was born into a family of bootleggers in Mississippi in 1930. After encountering horrendous racism and the murder of his brother in 1946, Perkins fled to California in 1947. There he became financially comfortable, married and began a family. In 1957 Perkins met Christ through his young son's attendance at a Bible class.

As Perkins grew in Christ, he and his wife, Vera Mae, eventually recognized that God was calling them back to Mississippi. So they returned and established Voice of Calvary Ministries. In Mississippi they encountered strong opposition. At one point

Perkins and others were beaten brutally by police officers. Yet through all of this Perkins remained steadfast in his vision and action. All that he did is explicable only on the basis of the gospel, as he testifies:

> God made his love visible to the world in the person of Jesus Christ. And Jesus Christ made his love visible to the world in his unselfish death on the cross for our sin. So it becomes our responsibility as the Body of Christ to so live out his life on earth as to make the love of God visible in our time.[21]

Today the ministries that Perkins established in Mississippi and other places stand as vital witnesses to the gospel by embodying evangelical love.

To witness to the gospel we need love as a virtue. No principle, no law, can tell us how to respond with love in all situations. Only people who are habituated in the gospel virtue of love have the ability to discern the appropriate way of acting in love. By habituating us in love the gospel transforms us into people who are capable of responding to others in accordance with the gospel.

Doing as evangelical. We live in the midst of a cultural situation that continually undermines our habituation in love as the Christian way of doing. Modernity constantly teaches people to treat others as means to an end or as ends in themselves.[22] But the virtue of love as evangelical habituates the disciple community in the gospel as the end, the eschaton. So our doing, if it is to be evangelical, must always be guided by the claims of the everlasting reality of the gospel. It is the gospel that habituates us in love for others, not others that habituate us in love, and it is the gospel's claim on our lives that calls us to love our enemies, not the claim of our enemies.

This subtle distinction guides our self-giving. If we are habituated in evangelical love, then our self-giving is for the sake of the gospel, not for the sake of others. If we do not make this distinction, the life of self-giving simply puts our life at the disposal of others. We become in effect doormats, servants of the desires of others. But the desires of others are not always shaped by the gospel. Therefore we must undergo the rigorous training of habituation in the gospel, so that the virtue of love is not corrupted into a weak spinelessness but is instead a disciplined and faithful witness to the gospel.

This distinction also helps us resist the corruption of love threatened by postmodernity. Postmodernity exposes all human acting as expressions of the will to power. We succumb to the corruption of postmodernity when we act as if love is the way Christians gain power over others. When we think and act as if love is the way to win over our enemies, we have succumbed to the corruption of the will to power. When we think that acting in love is somehow the way to establish peace in this world, we have succumbed to the postmodern temptation.[23]

Actions that are guided by our habituation in love are not the exercise of power by "Christian" means. Love is not the way to exercise power as the disciple community, nor is love the way to make this world peaceable. Rather, love is the way the disciple community lives in and witnesses to the peaceableness of the eschaton revealed in the gospel. If this world is not redeemed by God in Christ, then love is not a virtue to be desired. But if we know that God redeems the world in Christ and if we participate in that redemption, then gospel-shaped love is the only way to live in this world as witness to that redemption.

Love as spiritual. The virtue of love by which we are habituated in the gospel is not only evangelical, it is also spiritual. By *spiritual* I mean that the virtue of love is formed in us by the work of the Holy Spirit. This does not mean that the virtue of love is spiritual as opposed to physical. It means that our entire life, our entire being, is transformed by the work of the Spirit so that we are able to act in love.

The first work of the Holy Spirit in habituating us in love is the killing of our old way of life. Paul asserts that "if you live according to the flesh, you will die; but if by the Spirit you put to death the deeds of the body, you will live" (Rom 8:13). This verse teaches four things.

First, apart from the work of Christ and the Holy Spirit our being is marked by death. Although Paul describes dying in the future tense here, in other places he asserts that our present lives are already marked by death (Rom 8:10; Eph 2:1). So the *telos* of life apart from Christ is death, and that *telos* shapes our life today apart from Christ.

Second, we live only by putting to death "the deeds of the body." We can understand this statement only if we consider Paul's use of *body* (Greek *sōma*) and *flesh* (Greek *sarx*). These terms have been the source of much debate in the church, but scholars generally agree that Paul uses *body* to refer to our physical bodies and *flesh* to refer to our sinful nature. In Romans 8:13 *body* is not simply another word for *flesh,* it is the means by which we sin. As Robert Gundry argues,

> The deeds of the body have their immediate source in the *soma,* but their ultimate source in the *sarx,* which dominates the *soma* and is thereby distinguishable from it.
>
> Thus, "put to death the deeds of the body" means "put to death the deeds worked out through the body under the influence of the flesh." . . . Hence only [the body's] deeds done under the influence of the flesh become the object of mortification.[24]

In this text, then, Paul tells us that we live only as we die to our old way of life.

Third, *we* are called to act *by the Spirit*. The conjunction of our acting and the Spirit's power is not one we can disentangle.[25] But the call for us to act does reinforce the insight, drawn from virtue ethics, that the Christian life is one in which we are transformed. At the same time this text also teaches that we cannot transform ourselves by our own power. By the power of the Spirit the old life which is incapable of love is put to death so that a new being and a new way of life may be formed in us.

Therefore the Spirit that habituates us in the virtue of love also gives us new life. The gospel does not simply call us to die, it calls us to die so that new life can be born in us. This new life is the work of the Spirit, and it is also our life. Since this new life is given by God through the Spirit of Christ, it is marked by habituation in the love revealed by Christ. As we are habituated in love by the Spirit, we have no need to protect our lives. We live by the power of the Spirit, not by the power that we obtain from others and exercise over others.

The self-giving of the disciple community then is simply the "sacrifice" of the old way of life and the realization of this new life. It is our living witness to Jesus' proclamation that "those who try to make their life secure will lose it, but those who lose their life will keep it" (Lk 17:33).

Finally the work of the Spirit in killing and giving life is a work of transformation. The particularities that mark us as persons are not simply erased by the Spirit, they are transformed. This entails the killing of all in us that is against God. But it does not mean that our abilities, our education, our history is merely canceled. It means that all that we are is redeemed so that all that we are becoming is formed in the new way of life in service to the gospel. When Paul became a servant of the gospel, God did not erase all that he had previously learned. Instead, God transformed it so that his rabbinic training and Roman citizenship empowered his service to the gospel as he was habituated in the virtue of love.

In the same way, John Perkins was shaped by love as spiritual. When Perkins was a child, the only use his bootlegging family had for Christians was to sell them moonshine. He "had always looked at black Christians as sort of inferior people whose religion had made them gullible and submissive."[26] So when Christ took hold of Perkins's life, the Spirit had to kill off that old life and give him a new one. At the same time, however, the Spirit transformed and redirected the ambition and abilities that had provided the Perkins family with a comfortable life in California and sent them back to the South in service to the gospel.

Doing as spiritual. As we are habituated in the virtue of love as spiritual, our way of doing is transformed so that we may be more faithful witnesses to the gospel in our cultural situation. Modernity teaches us to act in order to make our life secure. In this sense, the whole project of modernity may be understood as an attempt to secure our lives without God's help. Over against this, the Christian way of doing asserts that our life is secure only as we give up our lives by the power of the Holy Spirit and receive life as a gift from God.

Postmodernity teaches that our lives are ineradicably marked by the quest for power and that this quest is inevitably characterized by violence and death. The virtue of love that is formed by the Spirit teaches us that postmodernists are half-right. Since by the Spirit we must put to death the old way of life, they are right in their exposure of life apart from God. But they are wrong to think that this is the end of the story, because by the power of the Spirit we are formed in a new life marked by the peaceableness and self-giving of love.

As long as we continue the modernist project of securing our own life, all our doing will be marked by death. As long as we accept the postmodernist conviction that death, not life, marks our being, all of our doing will be soaked in violence. When by the power of the Spirit we put to death the old way of life, we begin to be habituated in new life that is marked by the love that gives life.

Love as natural. As we put to death the old life and are raised to new life by the power of the Spirit, we are habituated in the virtue of love as natural. This may seem to contradict the claim that love is spiritual. But if we understand that by the Spirit we are made new beings, then we can see how the virtue of love is natural.

Although the virtue of love is unnatural to life apart from Christ, when we are in Christ the virtue of love is natural. To say that love is both spiritual and natural is to say that the Spirit creates in us new life that is naturally marked by love. That does not mean that the formation of love requires no effort. Just as our physical birth must be followed by effort in order for us to grow into that which is natural, so our spiritual birth must be followed by effort if we are to grow into that which is natural to our new life.

When we are in Christ and resist the work of the Spirit, we are fighting against our very nature. But when we cooperate with the work of the Spirit, we begin to realize our new nature. The conflict in which we are engaged as the Spirit habituates us in love is described well by Roberta Bondi:

> The very desire to love and be loved is part of human nature. It is part of the image of God. Loving is natural; it is unnatural not to love. Of course, most human beings fail to love or love badly a lot of the time. This is because we are dominated by the fear of death and of our own physical and emotional vulnerability, and by our ways of compensating for this fear. We need power over other people. We are afraid of the future. We suffer from envy, resentments, depression, hyperactivity, and boredom.[27]

The only way to overcome the fear of death and our ways of compensating for that fear is by dying to the unnatural life that is marked by those things. When we die to that unnatural life, then the love that is natural to our humanity begins to be formed in us. In other words, through habituation in the virtue of love we are becoming human for the first time in our lives.[28]

Doing as natural. When we are habituated in the virtue of love as natural, we are equipped to meet the challenges of our cultural situation. Modernity asserts that everything humans do is to be directed toward self-realization and self-assertion. As Bondi notes, we fail to love because we fear death. So our lives become attempts to overcome death and the vulnerability that reminds us of our death. In modernity then what is natural to humanity is the assertion of self against death. All our doing is meant to secure the self by our own efforts.

Over against modernity, the virtue of love teaches that such doing is the loss of our humanity, not its realization. Our self-doing is unnatural. We must unlearn what we have come to think of as natural if we are to learn the true nature of humanity and find ourselves in Jesus Christ. Doing for others in witness to the gospel is not the denial of our humanity but the discovery of our humanity.

In postmodernity all our self-doing is exposed as simply the will to power. Our fear of death finds its natural expression in the violence of our lives. Over against postmodernity, the virtue of love calls us to a new being, a new way of life, that is characterized by the peaceableness of love. Since our old self has been put to death and since our new self is the gift of God, we can unlearn our fear of death. What is natural for us in Christ is not the fear of death and violence but freedom from fear and freedom for peace.

Both modernity and postmodernity give strong accounts of what is natural for humanity. In the gospel we have another account of what is natural. As we are habituated in love, we are enabled to do what is natural for humanity as created and redeemed by God.

Love as communal. As we are habituated in the virtue of love as evangelical, spiritual and natural we are also habituated in love as communal. This is a stronger claim than it may first appear to be. When I say that love is communal, I am not merely saying that love creates the possibility of our living in community. Nor am I merely saying that communities help sustain love. Rather, I am saying that being habituated in love is synonymous with community. Since we have learned to think of ourselves as individuals who form community by our own choices, this claim needs further development.

Under the influence of modernity, we may think of the virtue of love as something that transforms individuals into people who are free to form a community and capable of sustaining that community. Over against this, I am asserting that becoming a participant in the disciple community is simultaneous with being habituated in love. We cannot be habituated in love and then decide whether or not to become part of the disciple community. We are habituated in love only as we are members of the disciple community.

This knowledge of love as communal has been one of the marks of John Perkins's ministry from the very beginning. When he and his family returned to Mississippi in 1959, they began to develop a community that could sustain witness to the gospel. This community eventually developed a host of ministries that could not have been established by individuals alone. As they faced pressure and persecution, they needed each other to keep them on the path of love that witnesses to the gospel. In *With Justice for All* Perkins describes the actions that are necessary to "Christian community development,"[29] and he has given the later years of his life entirely to this ministry of Christian community development. Perkins knows and teaches that gospel-shaped love is communal.

This love-in-community embodies our participation in Christ. In his prayer in John 17, Jesus asks that we may live in him and he in us. He goes on to pray "on behalf of those who will believe in me through their word, that they may all be one. As you, Father, are in me and I am in you, may they also be in us, so that the world may believe that you have sent me" (vv. 20-21). The unity called on in this prayer is first of all the unity-in-love of God's own life. In the trinitarian relationship of Father, Son and Holy Spirit, God lives in love. God's acting in love toward creation is an extension of this life toward us. When we are incorporated into Christ, we become participants in this love. That does not mean that we become God. It means that as humans we become participants in the community of love.

Although I will devote the next chapter to a description of one practice of this community-in-love, I will here note that since it is formed in love, its life is characterized by the virtue of love. This means that the disciple community is evangelical, spiritual and natural. In order to be evangelical, its life must be one of action, sacrifice and responsiveness. In order to be spiritual, it must continually put to death the way of living that marks this world and receive its life, its very being, as a gift of God through the Holy Spirit. In order to be natural, it must continually grow into new life in Jesus Christ.

Doing as communal. At this point we should have a fairly clear understanding of the witness to the gospel embodied in love as communal. As this love guides our way of doing, it presents a radical challenge to our cultural situation. One of the pillars of modernity is the primacy of the individual.[30] With few exceptions, the political history of the modern world is built on the freedom of the individual to choose his own associations. Community then is something created by individuals.

Against this modernist doctrine and practice, love as communal proclaims the primacy, indeed, the necessity of community for human life. Just as the kidney, for example, does not have a life of its own and cannot decide whether or not to join with other organs to form a body, so each of us in the body of Christ lives only as we are joined together. According to the gospel, we become human only as we participate in community, in a particular community formed by God's redemptive work. So contrary to modernity, we do not find ourselves and then form community, we find ourselves as we are habituated in love, which is community.

In postmodern society the self is effaced, and we are left only with "communities" that are at war with each other. Since this is one of the most radical changes from modernity, most of us still have difficulty thinking in terms of the erasure of the individual.

Nevertheless, this is the "promise" of postmodernity. Against the effacement of the self, the virtue of love declares that we find our true selves only as persons-in-community, where we do what is natural for humanity—love. Against the warring communities of postmodernity, the virtue of love is the formation of the community of new humanity that is marked by peaceableness rather than by violence.

As we acknowledge these claims of the gospel on the disciple community, we are also driven to confess that we continually fail. Such confession is itself a witness to the gospel and our participation in the gospel by the forgiveness of God in God's loving work of redemption. It is also a reminder of how often we have been formed not by the gospel but by the world. Such confession, finally, is a call to recommit our lives as a disciple community to being formed in the virtue of love as communal.

Conclusion

Although our culture trivializes love and trades it for the trappings of power, we cannot abandon the virtue of love. It stands at the very heart of the gospel. In the good news of redemption in Jesus Christ, God is revealed as love. If we in the disciple community are to witness faithfully to Jesus Christ, we must be habituated in love. Left to our own devices, we turn love into hate. But by the power of the Spirit, we die to the rule of death and violence and live in the kingdom of life and peace. That life is made possible by Jesus Christ, who refused to confront hate with hate and violence with violence. Instead he acted in love and continues to act today, forming a new humanity, habituated in love, that stands as witness to the world of God's eschatological redemption.

Eight

TEACHING LOVE

The Practice of Hospitality

· · · · · · · · · · · · · · · · · · · ·

FOR ALMOST AS FAR BACK AS I CAN REMEMBER, OUR FAMILY ALWAYS had someone living with us. My maternal grandmother lived with us for many years. After her death our "spare" bedroom was home to a succession of homeless young people, visiting missionaries and friends who needed temporary help. As far as I know, we never rented the room. People contributed to household expenses as they were able.

As my sister and I grew into our teen years, our home became a center of activity. We seldom ate dinner alone as a family, and our guests were not always planned. In recent years I have come to realize that without fanfare my parents practiced hospitality throughout their lives. That's the way it is with the practice of hospitality. If someone really makes his or her home your home, there really is nothing spectacular about it.

Many of our congregations have "hospitality committees" that are responsible for providing food at various events and perhaps arranging housing for a visiting missionary or choir. We may be tempted to think that their work is rather mundane and trivial, but I will argue that this practice of hospitality goes to the heart of the gospel. When we understand hospitality as a practice of the gospel, it is one of the primary means by which we learn and teach love.

I will begin by considering hospitality as a practice in the church. Since we tend to trivialize hospitality and do not think of hospitality as a practice equal to education and worship, I will take some time to establish the significance of hospitality. Then I will seek to expose some of the characteristics of our cultural situation that corrupt the practice of hospitality and that offer opportunities for faithful witness to the gospel through its practice. Finally I will give an account of the practice of hospitality that teaches us the virtue of love.

The Significance of Hospitality

The practice of hospitality in Scripture. The practice of hospitality receives strong commendation in the Old Testament:

> You shall not oppress a resident alien; you know the heart of an alien, for you were aliens in the land of Egypt. (Ex 23:9)
>
> When an alien resides with you in your land, you shall not oppress the alien. The alien who resides with you shall be to you as a citizen among you; you shall love the alien as yourself, for you were aliens in the land of Egypt. I am the LORD your God. (Lev 19:33-34)

Here Israel's practice of hospitality reflects their own history and their relationship to God.

In the New Testament this practice continues. Paul instructs the Roman church to "contribute to the needs of the saints; extend hospitality to strangers" (Rom 12:13). In his letters to Timothy and Titus, Paul lists the practice of hospitality as one of the qualifications of a bishop (1 Tim 3:2; Tit 1:8). Peter instructs the church to "be hospitable to one another without complaining" (1 Pet 4:9), and the author of Hebrews tells us to "let mutual love continue. Do not neglect to show hospitality to strangers, for by doing that some have entertained angels without knowing it" (13:1-2, a reference to Gen 18).

Today, although we continue to practice something that we call *hospitality,* we seldom understand its centrality to our life in the gospel. In part this is because we simply have not taken the time to reflect on it, but it is also rooted in characteristics of our life as a church and in our larger cultural setting. Later I will examine this cultural resistance to hospitality, but here I will identify some aspects of the life of the church that undermine our practice of hospitality.

Obstacles to the practice of hospitality. One obstacle is the church's prosperity. Most churches in the West today are still prosperous enough that people do not need each other's hospitality. Many go out together to a restaurant for a meal instead of visiting each other's homes. The former may be a time of fellowship, but it is certainly not the practice of hospitality. Moreover, when we travel it is not often for purposes of ministry, and we are usually dependent on the "hospitality" of a motel chain, not other Christians.[1] The significance of hospitality in the Bible is often overlooked because Christians today are used to a travel guide full of places to eat and stay, whereas in the ancient Mediterranean world travelers had to depend on the hospitality of others.

Our prosperity may also undermine the practice of hospitality by enabling us to meet the needs of others without actually having to encounter them. One way we may do this is by giving money to other ministries. Prosperity in itself is not a bad thing, and giving is an important discipline that the church has always practiced. Nevertheless, we must be aware of the dangers. We should support institutionalized ministries, but as John Chrysostom concluded in the fourth century, that is not "a way of relieving individual Christians from their own duty to exercise hospitality."[2] Hospitality is not simply providing for the needs of others, it is the practice of welcoming others into our home by making our home their home.

The second obstacle to the practice of hospitality is the church's status. In the West the church has longed played a dominant role in culture. As a result the life and success of the church may appear to lie within our own power. When we believe this, we forget that our life is not our own and that we have no need or right to secure the life of the church for ourselves.

In this forgetfulness we engage in quests for status and security that undercut the practice of hospitality. We turn "community" into a means of protecting ourselves from others rather than connecting with them.[3] We do not want in our lives others who may threaten our status and security. Or if we do open our lives, it is in condescension, not hospitality. Christine Pohl argues that

> it is, in part, the hosts' own sense of vulnerability that allows them to offer recognition and respect to other vulnerable persons. Friendship, solidarity, and commensality occur among equals, and this requires an appreciation for what the guest might bring to the relationship. Persons who have never experienced need or marginality find it easier to be hosts than guests, and the deepest condescension may be expressed in their unwillingness to be a guest, an unwillingness to allow the relationship to be mutual.[4]

As our culture moves the church toward the margins of society, we may rediscover this practice of hospitality. But we should not wait for that to happen. Instead, we should recognize that the gospel itself teaches us our marginality and undergirds the practice of hospitality.

The third obstacle to the church's practice of hospitality is social structure. Social structures tend to be a means of identifying differences among us, such as race, class, age, sex.[5] No doubt there are good reasons for organizing some activities of the church on the basis of social structures, but when they dominate the life of the church they undercut the possibility of our learning love through the practice of hospitality. If we are only with people who are like us, then we will not be prepared to welcome strangers, people who are other than we are. Moreover, when we are together in the church on the basis of our social identity, we lose sight of the truth that our deepest source of identity is our togetherness in Christ.

In Jesus Christ, God set aside prosperity and status in order to welcome us in love into his family. In Jesus Christ, God became something alien to himself—he became human. If God in love can destroy those barriers and cross that divide, a divide deeper and wider and higher than any social structure, then we who are disciples of Jesus Christ must, and by God's grace can, learn to cross the barriers that divide us. Through the practice of hospitality our habituation in gospel-shaped love may begin.

Why We Need the Practice of Hospitality

In our Western culture, marked by the conflicts of modernity and postmodernity, the practice of hospitality is difficult to find and nearly impossible to imagine. Yet the world desperately needs the church's practice of hospitality as witness to the gospel of Jesus Christ.

Modernity's stress on the dominance of individualism and the quest for autonomy has turned us all into strangers.[6] In this situation, as Henri Nouwen reminds us,

> the movement from hostility to hospitality is hard and full of difficulties. Our society seems to be increasingly full of fearful, defensive, aggressive people anxiously clinging to their property and inclined to look at their surrounding world with suspicion, always expecting an enemy to suddenly appear, intrude and do harm.[7]

If my "self" is all that I have and all that really counts, then everything else is an enemy. As a result modernity is marked by our attempts to control others and protect ourselves.

In this situation the practice of hospitality can easily be corrupted into a means of control. Just as we must not think of love as the Christian way to power, we must not think of hospitality as the Christian way of controlling others. The practice of hospitality that is rooted in the love of the gospel is a dangerous practice. It surrenders control and takes risks.[8] If we succumb to the corruption of modernity our hospitality becomes another method of controlling others rather than being our witness to the gospel.

In contrast to modernity, postmodernity corrupts the practice of hospitality by its emphasis on communities.[9] At first this emphasis may appear to be a helpful move toward hospitality. However, the postmodern community simply displaces the individual. The characteristics of the individual in modernity—the insecurities, fears, violence and hostility—become characteristics of the community in postmodernity. As a result postmodern communities are no more capable of hospitality than are the modern individuals.

In cultural situations marked by postmodernity, we in the disciple community must unlearn its insecurities, fears, violence and hostility as we are habituated in love. Through the practice of hospitality, this process takes place as we surrender our quest for security and recognize that we live and act by God's grace. Through hospitality the Spirit forms in us the love that casts out all fear. Through hospitality we break the cycle of violence and hostility in our life. We are not guaranteed protection in this world. But then our life is eschatological—it is our participation in a new world as the new humanity, not our survival and success in this world.

This fear and hostility that enervates the practice of hospitality pervades our cultural situation. We can see it in our debates about immigrants, about multilingual education, about AIDS and about health care in general.[10] One of the strangest developments and greatest opportunities for the church in the West is the almost total absence of hospitality in hospitals.[11]

When hospitals were first established, their purpose was closer to our present-day hospices. Hospitals were places where the sick and dying were cared for. There was little that could actively be done to cure patients. All that could be given was care. Caregivers themselves often died as a result of their work, and the work was financially draining. Today we believe that we have failed if we do not cure patients, and many of those who work at curing patients live some of the most privileged lives in our society. Today one of the first questions hospitals ask is how we will pay for their services. So in spite of the goodwill of many who go into medicine, hospitals strongly resist any attempt to practice hospitality.

This situation reveals some of the worst aspects of our cultural situation. Patient care is measured in economic terms. When we cannot control life by curing a patient, we want to control life by determining the moment and manner of death. As managed care grows we are becoming special-interest communities, with consumer groups, medical associations and "health maintenance organizations" all pitted against one another.

In this situation the church has a wonderful opportunity to witness to the gospel. What if, through the generous giving of ability, training and money, the church provided an alternative to contemporary hospitals? What if churches banded together to provide health care and insurance for their members? At one time hospitals were the ministry of various churches. Could we recover that today? Although the questions and complexities are daunting, I think they are worth asking. I am not sure what such a practice would look like, but I am convinced that it would be an exhilarating participation in, and faithful witness to, the gospel.[12]

The Practice of Hospitality

As we practice hospitality we are habituated in the virtue of love that stands at the very heart of the gospel. Since we have trivialized and distorted hospitality, we do not often think of it as reflecting the heart of the gospel, but we should.[13] Hospitality reflects the love of the gospel through the practice of hospitality as evangelical, spiritual, natural and communal.

Hospitality as evangelical. Reflecting first on the language of the gospel will help us to understand how the practice of hospitality is gospel-shaped. In the gospel Jesus teaches that God is our "Father." We learn to call Jesus our "brother" and to think of ourselves as members of "God's family." All of this is the language of profound hospitality. We are not merely treated as if we are members of the family, we are *made* members of the family.

This reality is celebrated by one of the best-known and most-loved psalms:

You prepare a table before me
　in the presence of my enemies;
you anoint my head with oil;
　my cup overflows.
Surely goodness and mercy shall follow me
　all the days of my life,
and I shall dwell in the house of the LORD
　my whole life long. (Ps 23:5-6)

In the Old Testament the experience of Israel is that they are welcomed by God and given a home. As the passages describing the treatment of aliens remind Israel, they too were once aliens and homeless before God made them a people and gave them a home (Ex 23:9; Lev 19:33-34). In Psalm 23 the climax comes as the psalmist celebrates the hospitality of God.

In the New Testament this experience of Israel is filled to overflowing by the coming of Jesus Christ. The language that we have already considered depends for its meaning and power on the reality of God's redemption in Jesus Christ. In him we see the full meaning of hospitality. Through his life, death and resurrection we are welcomed by God:

He was in the world, and the world came into being through him; yet the world did not know him. He came to what was his own, and his own people did not accept him. But to all who received him, who believed in his name, he gave power to become children of God, who were born, not of blood or of the will of the flesh or of the will of man, but of God. (Jn 1:10-13)

This passage is filled with the language of hospitality and teaches us a number of things about evangelical hospitality.

First, this passage depicts the reversal of the guest-host relationship. We think of Jesus Christ as a guest in our world, but he turns out to be our host. He is the creator of this world, and it belongs to him. Thus the hospitality that is extended to us by God is an unshakable one because it is the hospitality of the creator of life. There is then no power that can overthrow our welcome. The disciple community is free from all the anxieties and fears that drive our hostility.

Second, this passage shows that the world is incapable of hospitality. The crucifixion was the ultimate act of our hostility—we crucified our host, the very source of our life. This teaches us that to practice hospitality we must be changed.[14] It also teaches us that hospitality is not without risks. Neither love nor hospitality are methods for ending all hostility in this world. They are not methods for turning all our enemies into friends. Rather, they are ways by which we witness to the gospel in a hostile world. We are not above our master—like him we will endure suffering, persecution and even death as we learn love through the practice of hospitality.

Third, this passage reminds us that God comes to us as a stranger.[15] Our Creator came to us and we did not recognize him. Only a few welcomed him at his birth, only a few followed him in his life, even fewer were with him at his death, and in his resurrection we still had difficulty recognizing him.

Typical of our difficulty is the experience of the two disciples on the road to Emmaus (Lk 24:13-35). As they are walking to Emmaus, downcast after the crucifixion, the resurrected Jesus joins them. They do not recognize him at first, but after walking and talking together for a while they invite this stranger to stay with them. As they are seated at the table, Jesus breaks bread and gives it to them: "Then their eyes were opened, and they recognized him" (v. 31). Only in their practice of hospitality and in Jesus' turning them from hosts to guests were these disciples given the ability to recognize him as their resurrected Lord.

The significance of welcoming Jesus as a stranger is given further weight by Jesus' story of judgment in Matthew 25:31-46. Jesus says that he comes to us in the guise of the hungry, the thirsty, the stranger, the naked, the sick and the imprisoned. When we welcome them, we welcome Jesus.[16] When we do not welcome them, we reject Jesus.

In these passages then we learn that hospitality is at the very heart of the gospel. In that gospel Jesus Christ comes to us and gives himself in death so that we may be welcomed into God's family. If in the gospel God comes to us as a stranger, then when we practice hospitality we learn to see Jesus and we welcome him in the guise of the stranger.

All this comes together for the church in our practice of Communion (or Eucharist). In that celebration we gather for one of the most significant expressions of hospitality—eating together. Jesus himself is our host at this meal. Our Creator and Redeemer welcomes us and feeds us.[17] In this meal, made possible by Christ's death, we learn that if God can welcome us and eat with us, our own practice of hospitality cannot exclude even those who would kill us.

So our practice of hospitality, if it is to inculcate the virtue of love, must be gospel-shaped—that is, it must participate in the story of God's redemption of creation through Jesus Christ. It must have no other aim than the joyous proclamation of the gospel that frees us from anxiety, fear, violence and hostility so that we may give our lives for others just as Christ gave his life in love for the world.

Evangelical hospitality teaches that the others for whom we may be called to give our lives might be strangers to us, might indeed be our enemies. We may find it easy to contemplate welcoming those who look like us, dress like us, sound like us and smell like us, but the stranger and the enemy are not those who are like us. They may be the homosexual AIDS patient, the struggling immigrant or the political refugee.

When I was pastoring a small church in an urban area of western Canada, we slowly learned the practice of evangelical hospitality. At the close of my ministry there our church included English-speaking Caucasians from Canada and the United States, Québecois, Native Canadians, African-Americans, Indonesian Chinese, Hong Kong Chinese, Chinese Canadians, Egyptian Copts and Ghanians. We had to work hard to overcome our misunderstandings and ignorance. At various times of the year we sought to learn about each other's cultures. At Christmas we sang songs in four or five languages. At potlucks we ate adventurously. At other times we struggled to understand one another.

As I look back on those years, I am convinced that one of the things that held so many different people together was our membership in God's family through the gospel. We belonged to each other because we belonged to God.

Hospitality as spiritual. As I noted in the previous chapter, the Spirit habituates us in love as we put to death our old way of life and are raised by the Spirit to new life in Christ. This same dynamic is described in John 1, where we are told that as long as we are in the "world" we cannot know Christ and that we become children of God by the will of God, not by any human power. So at the heart of our being welcomed by God's hospitality is this spiritual dynamic of dying and being raised.

This spiritual dynamic teaches us that the practice of hospitality will not come easily. It involves the pain of confronting and killing the habits and illusions of our old way of life. This process is not easy because we have been taught that the only "self" we have is the one formed by our old way of life. If the self that I have achieved is the only self that I have, then when I put it to death I am engaged in an act of self-immolation. But the gospel teaches that we have already been given new life, new selves in Christ, so dying to the old way of life is our new way of life.

Habituation in the hospitality of this new way of life requires great discipline. We need this discipline in order to live into the reality of God's love and hospitality. We also need it if we are to practice that hospitality in our own lives. But we must not make the mistake of thinking that learning God's hospitality and practicing our own hospitality are two separate things. Although God's welcome in Jesus Christ is the power and the criterion of our own practice, we learn that God loves us and welcomes us as we practice that love and welcome toward others.

This practice of welcoming others is itself an aspect of hospitality as spiritual. This spiritual dynamic of hospitality requires us to put to death our old way of life. But since that old way of life is so familiar to us and so deeply rooted in illusions about ourselves and the world, we do not find it easy to identify it. As we welcome those who are different from us through the practice of hospitality, they become gifts of the Spirit to help us see through our illusions and identify that old life. Stanley Hauerwas reminds us that this is not an easy process:

> The more successful we are at our deceptions—and the very fact that our deceptions always possess some truth means that we may be very successful in living them out—the more we feel the necessity to protect ourselves from any possible challenge. As a result we expand the circle of our friends very carefully because we intuitively know that we must not welcome any into our lives who might raise questions that challenge our illusions. Our "circle of friends" in fact becomes a conspiracy of intimacy to protect each of our illusions, particularly insofar as those illusions are the basis of what "peace" we might know. We thus fear the stranger who comes into our life uninitiated or unacquainted with "our way of thinking and doing things."[18]

Hauerwas's perceptive analysis helps us see why the practice of hospitality may be so painful and why we may not welcome the stranger. But if our practice of hospitality is rooted in the spiritual dynamic of dying and rising, we have no need to fear the stranger. Indeed, we then welcome the stranger, who helps us see through our deceptions so that we may die to them. We do not need to protect our own life because it is secure in Christ. We have no need to protect the false peace that is rooted in a conspiracy of illusion because we know that we have true peace in Christ.

So in contrast to modernity, the stranger is not someone that we must control or defeat. Instead, the stranger is one we welcome as a gift of the work of the Holy Spirit. In contrast to postmodernity, the "difference" of the "other" is not something that alienates us from him or her. Rather, the difference is a gift that helps us grow into new life.

This spiritual dynamic of God's hospitality also teaches us not to measure our practice of hospitality according to the worthiness of the stranger. When God welcomes us, he does not do so because we are worthy of hospitality: "God proves his love for us in that while we were still sinners Christ died for us" (Rom 5:8). If, while we were sinners and enemies, Christ reconciled us to God, then the hospitality of God's love does not depend on our worthiness. In the same way then our practice of hospitality as witness to the gospel cannot depend on the worthiness of others. Jesus exhorts us to this practice of hospitality:

> When you give a luncheon or a dinner, do not invite your friends or your brothers or your relatives or rich neighbors, in case they may invite you in return, and you would be repaid. But when you give a banquet, invite the poor, the crippled, the lame, and the blind. And you will be blessed, because they cannot repay you, for you will be repaid at the resurrection of the righteous. (Lk 14:12-14)

In calling us to this practice, Jesus calls us to the practice of hospitality that embodies the gospel.

Finally the spiritual dynamic of dying and rising teaches us to see ourselves in ways that further enable the practice of hospitality. First, it teaches that we are aliens in "the world" because that old way of life is alien to our humanity. That is why the old life must be killed for us to live. As we grow in new life in Christ, we come to understand more fully that we were once aliens when we lived apart from Christ. In the Old Testament Israel is to welcome the alien into their midst because they were once aliens (Ex 23:9; Lev 19:33-34). In the same way as the church we are to welcome the alien into our midst because we were once aliens.

Second, this spiritual dynamic teaches us to see ourselves as "marginal people." That is, as we grow into new life in Christ, we move away from the center of life in this world. As Christine Pohl has shown,

> historic and contemporary practices of Christian hospitality that involve more than entertainment of friends and family, that transcend prevailing social boundaries, build community, meet significant human needs, and reflect divine hospitality are associated with hosts who understand themselves in some way as marginal to the larger society.[19]

For the disciple community, this understanding of our marginality is rooted in our identity in the gospel as we die to life in the world and rise to life in Christ. As should be clear by now, this marginality is not an escape from our responsibility in the world. Rather, it is integral to faithful witness to God's eschatological redemption.

Hospitality as natural. As we are raised to new life by the Spirit, we enter into the practice of hospitality that is natural to that new life. Certainly the practice of hospitality still requires discipline on our part. But that practice is not a denial of our humanity—it is growth in the new humanity that is ours in Christ. As we are habituated in love, hospitality becomes something natural.

This is wonderfully demonstrated by the story of the French village of Le Chambon.[20] Le Chambon was a village of about three thousand. During World War II Le Chambon sheltered a large number of Jews from the Nazis. In spite of the dangers the villagers welcomed them into their homes and into their lives. Philip Hallie later visited the village in an effort to understand their actions:

I learned that the opposite of cruelty is not simply freedom from the cruel relationship; it is *hospitality*. . . . When I asked them why they helped these dangerous guests, they invariably answered, "What do you mean, 'Why?' Where else could they go? How could you turn them away? What is so special about being ready to help *(prête a servir)?* There was nothing else to do." And some of them laughed in amazement when I told them I thought they were "good people."[21]

In interactions with Hallie and in the interviews with villagers in the film *Weapons of the Spirit,* the villagers resist any suggestion that their actions were heroic or that they could have done otherwise. For them, the practice of hospitality was natural.

The people of Le Chambon, through their resistance to being thought of as heroic, destroy one of the deceptions that we use to avoid the claims of the gospel on our life. We tell ourselves that the gospel-shaped virtue of love and practice of hospitality are heroic accomplishments. Since we are ordinary people, we cannot—and surely God does not—expect heroic actions from us. The story of Le Chambon confronts us with ordinary people like us, formed in new life by the Holy Spirit, practicing the hospitality of the gospel as something natural to their life in Christ.

The practice of hospitality as the realization of that which is natural to our new life in Christ also guides the way we welcome the stranger in our midst. Henri Nouwen identifies this aspect of hospitality:

Hospitality . . . means primarily the creation of a free space where the stranger can enter and become a friend instead of an enemy. Hospitality is not to change people, but to offer them space where change can take place. It is not to bring men and women over to our side, but to offer freedom not disturbed by dividing lines. . . . Hospitality is not a subtle invitation to adopt the lifestyle of the host, but the gift of a chance for the guest to find his own.[22]

If our practice of hospitality is natural to our new life in Christ, then we will know that our mission is not to convert the other. Our mission is simply to witness to the gospel by providing this space for the Spirit to work and to lead others to the new life that is natural to humanity in Christ.

If we practice hospitality as something that is natural for the new humanity that is being formed in Christ, we will provide a powerful challenge to our cultural situation. According to modernity, the virtues are heroic and love is an extraordinary accomplishment. By God's grace the virtue of love and the practice of hospitality are natural to our lives, as they were to the lives of the Chambonnais. According to postmodernity, all that we do is marked by an agenda, by the will to power. In the church our love and hospitality are also often marked by our will to power. But for us, this will to power is not a sign of our humanity but of the incompleteness of that which is natural to our new humanity. Fear and violence are unnatural, love and hospitality are natural. So when our actions are marked by fear and violence, we do not accept or celebrate them. Rather, we confess them and receive God's forgiveness so that we may be free to love and to practice the hospitality of the gospel.

Hospitality as communal. The practice of hospitality that I have described here cannot be practiced by individuals—it must be communal.[23]

In the first place, the practice of hospitality simply *is* the formation of the disciple community. As Stephen Fowl and Gregory Jones note, "It is not a matter of first recovering a distinctive sense of Christian community and then asking about strangers, their needs, and the question of hospitality. Rather, as the New Testament makes abundantly clear, we discover Christian community *precisely in* showing hospitality to strangers."[24] That is because the disciple community is brought into being by the gospel, and the gospel is, at least in part, the practice of hospitality.

In the second place, community is necessary to sustain the practice of discipleship. We cannot take the kinds of risks that hospitality entails if we live apart from the support of a community. If we know that others in the community will be there to support us when we have needs, we can more easily risk what we have. In some situations this extends even further—we may risk our very lives because we know that others for whom we are responsible—children, spouses and other family members—will be cared for by the community.

In the third place, community is necessary for training in hospitality. As I have noted several times, hospitality, though it is natural to new life in Christ, is not easy to learn. In community we may be corrected and trained by others in this practice.

We may naturally think of the community that practices hospitality as a local community of those who live in close proximity. This kind of community will typically be most able to support our practice. But we should not restrict our thinking or our practice to geographical proximity. The presence through memory of my parents' practice of hospitality continues to nurture my own practice. Likewise, the "intellectual hospitality" that is offered to me by former teachers, colleagues and students has guided and sustained me in my own work.

Of course, the "community" that provides the most significant guide and sustenance for our practice of hospitality is Father, Son and Holy Spirit. Their perfect love and fellowship are certainly different from our struggle to be habituated in love and the practice of hospitality. But in their triune fellowship they represent to us the perfect eschatological communion toward which our life as humans is directed by the presence and power of the Holy Spirit through the reconciliation of Christ. As we participate in this eschatological redemption, we are able to put to death the fear and anxiety that fuel our divisions and our violence and grow in love and the practice of hospitality.

Conclusion

The village of Le Chambon provides a story of hospitality that summarizes much of this chapter. As Hallie observes, one of the reasons that the village was so prepared to offer hospitality is that it was largely inhabited by French Huguenots—Protestant Christians who through their early history in France had been hunted and killed and who during this century still remain marginal to French society. This experience of marginalization equipped these villagers to understand the gospel and the situation of the Jews.

Moreover, the villagers had as their pastor André Trocmé, who continually reminded them that when they welcomed a stranger they were welcoming Jesus. Particularly as they welcomed persecuted and hunted Jews, they could identify their guests with Jesus' own life. As they lived out this reminder, the villagers of Le Chambon simply witnessed to the gospel by which their own life was sustained.

Finally, their practice was natural to them. "For these villagers, repentance in the sense of a return to their fullest selves before God was simply a way of life."[25] By the Spirit they were putting to death the fears and violence of the old self and were living the life of the new humanity in Christ.

Most of us in the church in western European cultures do not have the history, the teaching or the community that sustained the love and hospitality of Le Chambon. But we do have the same gospel and the same Spirit at work among us. If we will commit ourselves to habituation in love and to the practice of hospitality, the God who loves us and welcomes us in Christ will be faithful and will make us faithful witnesses of the gospel in the midst of a fearful and violent world.

Conclusion
Toward Greater Faithfulness in Uncertain Times

The biblical authors, under the guidance of the Holy Spirit, are continually concerned with discerning the path of faithfulness for God's people. The books of the Pentateuch teach us the faithfulness of God in the midst of oppression and the unfaithfulness of his people as he calls them into being. When we consider them carefully, we see that the historical books of the Old Testament, which in the Hebrew canon are grouped together as "The Former Prophets," prophetically discern the faithfulness and unfaithfulness of the leaders and the people of Israel. "The Latter Prophets," Isaiah through Malachi, engage this task of discernment in ways that are even more obvious. The other books of the Old Testament, the "Writings" in the Hebrew canon, also teach us to see God at work.

The New Testament continues this tradition of prophetic discernment. The Gospels and the Acts of the Apostles describe God's work through Christ in calling into being a new people, made up of Jews and Gentiles. In the letters of the New Testament the apostles continue this work by helping the new people of God discern the path of faithfulness in the midst of their cultural situations.

Although I would never lay claim to prophethood, I have sought in this book to continue that tradition. In order to discern the path of faithfulness for the people of God today, I have used the language of virtue. My description of the gospel virtues and practices has as its aim greater faithfulness on the part of God's people.

Faith, hope and love are the central virtues of the gospel.

Although I have treated them separately here, each exists in dependence on the others. Our way of knowing that comes by faith sustains and gives direction to our hope and our love. Our hope and love are gospel-shaped only if we know Christ by faith. Hope, in turn, embodies the way of living in light of what we come to know by faith. Gospel-shaped love is possible in this world only if our lives are rooted in the hope of the eschaton. Love then binds together faith and hope as we act in faithfulness to the gospel.

The practices of education, worship and hospitality shape these three virtues and are, in turn, shaped by them. But the relationships between these practices and virtues is not so neat as my description might imply. The practice of education forms hope and love, as well as faith. Likewise, in worship we are not just sustaining hope, we are also forming faith and learning love. As we learn love through the practice hospitality, we are further formed in faith and sustained in hope.

Of course, there are other gospel virtues and other practices of the church. But these give us the shape and foundation of those other virtues and practices. As we are habituated in faith, hope and love through education, worship and hospitality, our new being will be lead naturally to other virtues and practices that further enable faithful witness to the gospel in our time.

We live in uncertain times—at the end of modernity and the rise of postmodernity. But our times are no more uncertain or threatening than other times in which the disciple community has lived. And the God who enabled them to discern their unfaithfulness and restored them to faithful witness is still with us today.

What we need today are not better lives but new lives, not a more moral society but a more faithful church. My prayer is that this book will be one means by which God will form new life and enable us to be more faithful as witnesses to the good news of Jesus Christ, which is the redemption of the world.

Notes

Chapter 1: The Rising Popularity of Virtue

[1] Alasdair MacIntyre, *After Virtue: A Study in Moral Theory*, 2nd ed. (Notre Dame, Ind.: University of Notre Dame Press, 1984); Stanley Hauerwas, *Character and the Christian Life: A Study in Theological Ethics*, 2nd ed. (San Antonio, Tex.: Trinity University Press, 1984).

[2] The relationship between Aristotle and Christian theology is complex. In the Middle Ages, St. Thomas Aquinas sought to synthesize Aristotle and Christian theology in his *Summa Theologiae* (or *Summa Theologica*). Today Aristotle's account continues to give guidance, at least in spirit and form if not in substance, to Christian virtue ethics. At the same time, however, Aristotle and the gospel have different conceptions of the good, different communities and different virtues. So any Christian synthesis of Aristotle and the gospel seeks in the end to transform Aristotle's account, which may be found in his *Nicomachean Ethics*.

Helpful studies of Aristotle include Amelie Rorty, ed., *Essays on Aristotle's Ethics* (Berkeley: University of California Press, 1980); MacIntyre, *After Virtue;* and Nancy Sherman, *The Fabric of Character: Aristotle's Theory of Virtue* (Oxford: Clarendon, 1989). For theological consideration of Aristotle's account, see Hauerwas, *Character and the Christian Life*, chap. 2; John Milbank, *Theology and Social Theory: Beyond Secular Reason* (Oxford: Basil Blackwell, 1990), chap. 11; and Stanley Hauerwas and Charles Pinches, *Christians Among the Virtues: Theological Conversations with Ancient and Modern Virtues* (Notre Dame, Ind.: University of Notre Dame Press, 1997), chaps. 1-3. For a brief discussion of Thomas Aquinas, see "Heroic Virtue and Christian Virtue" in chapter two.

[3] Gilbert Meilaender, *The Theory and Practice of Virtue* (Notre Dame, Ind.: University of Notre Dame Press, 1984), pp. 4-5.

[4] This is a very rough summary of the two dominant approaches to ethics in our culture—deontological and consequentialist (of which utilitarianism is the most prevalent form). For further bibliography and discussion of these approaches, see the standard introductions by William K. Frankena, *Ethics*, 2nd ed. (Englewood Cliffs, N.J.: Prentice-Hall, 1973), and Arthur F. Holmes, *Ethics: Approaching Moral Decisions* (Downers Grove, Ill.: InterVarsity Press, 1984).

[5] By "traditional" ethics I do not mean the popular notion of ethics. Rather, by "traditional" I mean the approach to ethics that has come to predominate among thoughtful people in our culture. Of course, virtue ethics also

has a long tradition—stretching all the way back to Plato and Aristotle. In order to emphasize these different uses of *traditional,* I will put "traditional" in quotes when I am referring to the dominant view of ethics in our culture.

[6]Expressing the same concern, Hauerwas and Pinches *(Christians Among the Virtues)* caution that "it is important for us to say that while we use them freely, the new philosophical defenses of virtue are, for the most part, of little interest to us in themselves. This is so because we have absolutely no stake in defending virtue as a thing in itself. Indeed as we will try to show in this chapter, to defend virtue itself is a dangerous thing for Christians to do, for they may discover that the defense invariably yields a set of virtues that are vicious—that is, vicious according to the Christian gospel" (p. 55).

[7]What I have called *decisionism* has come under attack from a variety of directions (see Hauerwas and Pinches, *Christians Among the Virtues,* chap. 4, and Bernard Williams, *Ethics and the Limits of Philosophy* [Cambridge, Mass.: Harvard University Press, 1985]). The most sustained critique of the traditional account of ethics is found in MacIntyre, *After Virtue.*

[8]Philip P. Hallie's book *Lest Innocent Blood Be Shed: The Story of the Village of Le Chambon and How Goodness Happened There* (San Francisco: Harper & Row, 1980) and the film *Witness of the Spirit* are marvelous portrayals of the village of Le Chambon in just these terms. The portrayal of Oskar Schindler's character in Steven Spielberg's movie *Schindler's List* reminds us, by portraying the mixture of virtue and vice in Schindler's character, that virtue ethics does not guarantee easy, clear-cut analyses.

[9]Feminists have often criticized the tradition of virtue ethics for its patriarchalism (see Gloria Albrecht, *The Character of Our Communities: Toward an Ethic of Liberation for the Church* [Nashville: Abingdon, 1995]). Although the conversation between feminism and virtue ethics is far from conclusive, as I develop my account I will try to be sensitive to feminist criticisms, though I will not always note those points of sensitivity.

[10]See "Graces, Not Virtues" under "Theological Objections to Virtue Ethics" in chapter two.

[11]See "Community" under "The Gospel and Virtue Ethics" in chapter two.

[12]As we will see in the following chapters, an account of the Christian virtues of faith, hope and love seeks to protect us from accounts of the virtues that, for a Christian, are false and vicious. As Hauerwas and Pinches *(Christians Among the Virtues)* remind us, drawing on the work of John Milbank, "As founded on Christ, Christian virtue cannot but be teleologically oriented to peace, just as Greek virtue cannot but be ordered to war. . . . Christian virtue is not so much initiated action but response to a love relation with God in Christ" (p. 68). Milbank's argument may be found in his "Can Morality Be Christian?" in *The Word Made Strange: Theology,*

Language, Culture (Oxford: Basil Blackwell, 1997), pp. 219-32, and *Theology and Social Theory.*

[13]MacIntyre, *After Virtue,* pp. 51-61.

[14]The usual term for this in ethics is *emotivism.* See MacIntyre, *After Virtue,* chaps. 2 and 3. One contemporary expression of emotivism that pretends to be "ethical" is the program of "values clarification." This program is an almost pure example of the emotivist results of "traditional" ethics, but it does not concern itself with the good or, in the end, even with the right. "Values clarification" merely asks what the individual feels most strongly about. This is an abandonment of the moral in favor of the psychological.

[15]We will shortly examine how this dissatisfaction extends to the elevation of the rights of the individual over the life of a community.

[16]Although they disagree in some respects, the work of both Bill Bennett and Hillary Rodham Clinton take this approach. As a result, their similarities are at least as important as their differences.

[17]Both John Rawls and Richard Rorty are examples of this strategy. See Rawls's magisterial (but flawed) work *A Theory of Justice* (Cambridge, Mass: Belknap/Harvard University Press, 1971) and his more recent development of the argument in *Political Liberalism* (New York: Columbia University Press, 1993). For Rorty, see his "The Priority of Democracy to Philosophy," in *Objectivism, Relativism and Truth: Philosophical Papers* (Cambridge: Cambridge University Press, 1991), pp. 175-96.

[18]This is, of course, a controversial claim. Christians have long been willing to kill in the name of the gospel. Nevertheless, as I will seek to show throughout my account, Christian virtues and practices are rooted in and should embody the gospel of peace. That does not mean that they will bring an end to conflict, but it does mean that the life of the people who embody these virtues will more faithfully witness to the gospel.

[19]The most obvious turn to the community is found in the "communitarian movement" associated with thinkers such as Amitai Etzioni and Bill Bennett. As I will argue below, I do not think Christians should join this movement because it begs the question, What *kind* of community are we forming? Christians are committed to forming a specific community—the church—before their commitment to any other form of community.

[20]Reasoning about consequences does not have to be individualist. Indeed, the most influential form of ethical consequentialism—utilitarianism—has given us the rule "the greatest good for the greatest number" as a guide to morality. Here I am simply arguing that in our culture individualism, combined with duty or consequences, has led to an increasing dissatisfaction with traditional ethics.

[21]MacIntyre, *After Virtue,* pp. 239-43, 254-55, 262-63. See also Jonathan R. Wilson, *Living Faithfully in a Fragmented World: Lessons for the Church from MacIntyre's "After Virtue"* (Valley Forge, Penn.: Trinity Press, forth-

coming).

[22]MacIntyre, *After Virtue*, p. 263. See the criticisms of Hauerwas and Pinches in Wilson, *Living Faithfully in a Fragmented World*, pp. 91-97 (typescript), and their citation of the argument of Milbank, *Theology and Social Theory*, pp. 326-79. I should note that sometime after writing *After Virtue* MacIntyre returned to the church as the particular community in which he now seeks the virtuous life.

[23]Meilaender, *Theory and Practice of Virtue*, p. x, quoting Iris Murdoch.

[24]Ibid, pp. 13-17, 36-40. Meilaender draws on the work of Bernard Williams, "Utilitarianism and Moral Self-Indulgence," in *Contemporary British Philosophy*, ed. H. D. Lewis (London: George Allen & Unwin, 1976), pp. 306-21.

Chapter 2: Can Virtue Be Christian?

[1]The most prominent of these is St. Thomas Aquinas (1225?-1274). His magisterial *Summa Theologiae* (or *Summa Theologica*) contains much discussion of the virtues in conversation with Aristotle and others. The *Summa* is divided into three large parts. The entire second part, which is subdivided into two parts (I-II and II-II), considers the virtues in general and in detail.

[2]Karl Barth, *Church Dogmatics* 2/2 ("Doctrine of God"), trans. G. W. Bromiley et al., ed. G. W. Bromiley and T. F. Torrance (Edinburgh: T & T Clark, 1957), pp. 509-41.

[3]For an insightful treatment of Barth's ethics, see Nigel Biggar and the works he cites in *The Hastening That Waits: Karl Barth's Ethics*, Oxford Studies in Theological Ethics (Oxford: Clarendon, 1993). Barth has other contributions to make to our discussion below.

[4]Dietrich Bonhoeffer, *Ethics*, trans. Neville Horton Smith and ed. Eberhard Bethge (New York: Macmillan, 1965), p. 17: "The knowledge of good and evil seems to be the aim of all ethical reflection. The first task of Christian ethics is to invalidate this knowledge. In launching this attack on the underlying assumptions of all other ethics, Christian ethics stands so completely alone that it becomes questionable whether there is any purpose in speaking of Christian ethics at all. But if one does so notwithstanding, that can only mean that Christian ethics claims to discuss the origin of the whole problem of ethics, and thus professes to be a critique of all ethics simply as ethics."

[5]Donald G. Bloesch, *Freedom for Obedience: Evangelical Ethics for Contemporary Times* (San Francisco: Harper & Row, 1987), p. 81.

[6]Ibid., p. 191. See also Bloesch's discussion on pp. 22 and 81-83.

[7]Gilbert Meilaender, *The Theory and Practice of Virtue* (Notre Dame, Ind.: University of Notre Dame Press, 1984), p. x.

[8]Here I should note the centrality of forgiveness to Christian life and community, a practice that undergirds everything that I say here. We are

fortunate to have a superb account of forgiveness in L. Gregory Jones, *Embodying Forgiveness: A Theological Analysis* (Grand Rapids, Mich.: Eerdmans, 1995).

[9]John Milbank's account is guided by his conception of a Christian "ontology of peace." Although the reader may infer something about Milbank's ontology of peace from my discussion, I will not try to provide an account of it. Like Milbank, I am committed to an ontology of peace rooted in the gospel. I intend for that commitment to shape my account of the virtues and practices.

[10]See John Milbank's assertion that "Augustine charged the Romans with having no real virtue, because they knew no real peace—either at the level of practice, *or* at the level of mythological and ontological conception" (*Theology and Social Theory: Beyond Secular Reason* [Oxford: Basil Blackwell, 1990], p. 363). Milbank's explication and defense of Augustine's charge may be found on pp. 389-92.

[11]Milbank, *Theology and Social Theory*, p. 376: "The Christian *mythos* . . . is able to rescue virtue from deconstruction into violent, agonistic difference."

[12]Milbank, *Theology and Social Theory*, p. 359. Lest the reader be left with the impression that Milbank's critique is limited historically to the Greeks, let me note that, albeit briefly, he shows that the "Derridean deconstruction, or the Deleuzean reversal, of Platonism, both depend upon a dualism mediated by conflict that is already encoded by Platonism itself. This 'deeper' identity of Platonism they do not question, but merely reproduce as transcendental violence" (p. 376).

[13]This is not to deny the element of struggle in living the Christian life. Rather, it is to recognize that even the language of warfare in the Bible is guided by an ultimate recognition that God's work in Jesus Christ is the reconciliation and redemption of the world. For example, although the letter to the Ephesians makes much use of warfare language (6:10-17), its central theme is peace (2:11-22). Our "warfare," then, is a spiritual war against those things which keep us from living peaceably.

[14]*Prudentia* and *phronēsis* are intellectual acts by which we judge the prudent or practical thing to do in a particular instance.

[15]The literature on this controversy is extensive. See the works referred to in Stanley Hauerwas and Charles Pinches, *Christians Among the Virtues: Theological Conversations with Ancient and Modern Virtues* (Notre Dame, Ind.: University of Notre Dame Press, 1997), chap. 8, and Richard J. Mouw, *The God Who Commands* (Notre Dame, Ind.: University of Notre Dame Press, 1990). For an instructive debate over Barth's "divine command ethics," see Stanley Hauerwas, *Character and the Christian Life: A Study in Theological Ethics,* 2nd ed. (San Antonio, Tex.: Trinity University Press, 1984), William Werpehowski's two articles "Command and History in the

Ethics of Karl Barth," *Journal of Religious Ethics* 9 (1981): 298-320 and "Narrative and Ethics in Karl Barth," *Theology Today* 43, no. 3 (October 1986): 334-53, and Nigel Biggar and the works he cites in *The Hastening That Waits: Karl Barth's Ethics,* Oxford Studies in Theological Ethics (Oxford: Clarendon, 1993).

[16]One of the reasons that the language of virtue is superior to the language of divine command (one that I will not pursue in the text) is that much of the language of divine command ethics is determined today by the categories established by Immanuel Kant, and these categories are detrimental to an account of the Christian life. On this see Hauerwas and Pinches, *Christians Among the Virtues,* esp. chap. 8.

[17]This, of course, raises questions in light of the biblical naming of God as "Father." But as Hauerwas and Pinches (*Christians Among the Virtues,* chap. 8) show, even this language is suited to virtue ethics. For a helpful description of "friendship with God" as a central theme of Christian ethics, see L. Gregory Jones, *Transformed Judgment: Toward a Trinitarian Account of the Moral Life* (Notre Dame, Ind.: University of Notre Dame Press, 1990), chap. 2.

[18]Mouw, *The God Who Commands,* comes closest to the kind of account I have in mind.

[19]For similar accounts, see Stanley Hauerwas, *Character and the Christian Life,* Benjamin W. Farley, *In Praise of Virtue: An Exploration of the Virtues in a Christian Context* (Grand Rapids, Mich.: Eerdmans, 1995), and Joseph J. Kotva, Jr., *The Christian Case for Virtue Ethics* (Washington, D.C.: Georgetown University Press, 1996).

[20]Alasdair MacIntyre, *After Virtue: A Study in Moral Theory,* 2nd ed. (Notre Dame, Ind.: University of Notre Dame Press, 1984), chaps. 14 and 15.

[21]"Everlasting reality" is better than "living tradition" because it reminds us that the gospel is not a tradition that the church keeps alive but a reality that keeps the church alive.

[22]For this reason some have called the second volume of Luke's work, "the Acts of the Risen Lord through the Apostles by the Holy Spirit." Likewise, the letters of the New Testament discern how Jesus Christ continues to work among his followers.

[23]For some suggestions about the authority of Scripture, see Jonathan R. Wilson, "Toward a New Evangelical Paradigm of Biblical Authority," in *The Nature of Confession: Evangelicals and Postliberals in Conversation,* ed. Timothy R. Phillips and Dennis L. Ockholm (Downers Grove, Ill.: InterVarsity Press, 1996), pp. 151-61.

[24]Dietrich Bonhoeffer, *Ethics,* trans. Neville Horton Smith and ed. Eberhard Bethge (New York: Macmillan, 1965), p. 80.

[25]The statement on inerrancy may be found in *Inerrancy,* ed. Norman Geisler (Grand Rapids, Mich.: Zondervan, 1980). The disagreements on

man and woman are represented by differing positions of the Council on Biblical Manhood and Womanhood and Christians for Biblical Equality.

[26]Bonhoeffer, *Ethics,* pp. 81-82.

[27]See chapter five on the virtue of hope and chapter six on the practice of worship.

[28]In Thomas Aquinas the virtues enable us to live according to "natural law." The issues here are complex and considering them at length would take us away from my purpose. Suffice it to note here that if *natural law* is taken to mean that which we can know apart from the gospel, then we must reject this view of virtues and natural law. However, if *natural law* means that which God intended for this world and restores through the gospel, then we may accept this view of virtues and natural law. See the discussion of love as "natural" for redeemed humanity in chapter seven.

[29]I plan to enlarge this account in a future book, tentatively titled *Practicing Church.*

[30]MacIntyre, *After Virtue,* pp. 194-95.

[31]For an account of how the church may resist this corruption, see Jonathan R. Wilson, *Living Faithfully in a Fragmented World: Lessons for the Church from MacIntyre's "After Virtue"* (Valley Forge, Penn.: Trinity Press, forthcoming).

[32]"Set apart" is, of course, one of the primary convictions embodied in calling Christians "saints." By emphasizing this call, the emphasis on community in a Christian ethics of virtue also enables greater emphasis on the holiness to which we are called as disciples of Jesus Christ.

[33]Stanley Hauerwas, *The Peaceable Kingdom: A Primer in Christian Ethics* (Notre Dame, Ind.: University of Notre Dame Press, 1983), p. 100.

[34]MacIntyre *(After Virtue)* provides a rather lengthy definition of practice that will help us understand the special meaning of practices for virtue ethics: "By a 'practice' I am going to mean any coherent and complex form of socially established cooperative human activity through which goods internal to that activity are realised in the course of trying to achieve those standards of excellence which are appropriate to, and partially definitive of, that form of activity, with the result that human powers to achieve excellence, and human conceptions of the goods and ends involved, are systematically extended" (p. 187). MacIntyre's definition lies behind the account that I will give of the church's practices.

[35]In David S. Cunningham's recent work on the Trinity, *These Three Are One: The Practice of Trinitarian Theology* (Oxford: Basil Blackwell, 1998), he makes creative and insightful use of the virtues and practices. David and I have been friends for a long time, but we believe that we developed our approaches to these matters independently of each other.

[36]In Thomas Aquinas the theological virtues differ from the "intellectual virtues" and the "moral virtues." For Thomas, although these last two

categories of virtues may be present in us apart from God's grace, they are transformed in Christians by the theological virtues. This raises a number of interpretive issues regarding "acquired" and "infused" virtue that need not concern us here. For a discussion of these issues, see Romanus Cessario, O.P., *The Moral Virtues and Theological Ethics* (Notre Dame, Ind.: University of Notre Dame Press, 1991).

[37]For literature on modernity and postmodernity, see the references given at various points in the following chapters.

[38]Postmodernists point to the wars of the twentieth century, the most devastating in history, as proof of the violence of reason.

[39]The phrase *will to power* comes from Friedrich Nietzsche (1844-1900), the philosopher many regard as the first "postmodern" thinker. See Friedrich Nietzsche, *The Will to Power,* trans. Walter Kaufmann and R. J. Hollingdale, ed. Walter Kaufmann (New York: Random House, 1967). For Nietzsche as a postmodern thinker, see Stanley J. Grenz, *A Primer on Postmodernism* (Grand Rapids, Mich.: Eerdmans, 1996), pp. 88-98.

Chapter 3: Faith and the Christian Way of Knowing

[1]This is not to deny the "intellectual content" of the gospel or the importance of creeds and confessions of faith but to recognize the limitations of such statements, their proper role in pointing us to the gospel of Jesus Christ and the way that modernity may exercise a corrupting influence.

[2]I certainly want to affirm the biblical call to trust in Christ, but I want also to identify the way that postmodernity may corrupt that biblical call.

[3]The literature on postmodernity is voluminous and growing daily. (Scholars recognize a good thing when they see it!) I will refer to many works of postmodernity in the following discussion. For a good introductory survey of postmodern thought by an evangelical theologian, see Stanley J. Grenz, *A Primer on Postmodernism* (Grand Rapids, Mich.: Eerdmans, 1996). For a more critical evaluation of postmodernity by evangelicals, see Roger Lundin, *The Culture of Interpretation: Christian Faith and the Postmodern World* (Grand Rapids, Mich.: Eerdmans, 1993), and Gene Edward Veith, Jr., *Postmodern Times: A Christian Guide to Contemporary Thought and Culture* (Wheaton, Ill.: Crossway, 1994). For a variety of responses to postmodernity by evangelical theologians, see Timothy R. Phillips and Dennis L. Okholm, ed., *Christian Apologetics in the Postmodern World* (Downers Grove, Ill.: InterVarsity Press, 1995). For an insightful and entertaining introduction to postmodern approaches to biblical interpretation, see A. K. M. Adam, *What Is Postmodern Biblical Criticism?* (Philadelphia, Penn.: Fortress, 1995).

[4]By "European" cultures I mean both the cultures of Europe and those cultures outside Europe that have been significantly shaped by the European intellectual tradition.

[5]I must emphasize that the position I am taking seeks to grant authority to the gospel. Although new circumstances and new experiences may lead to new insights into the gospel, they are precisely that—new insights into the gospel. In other words, they are discoveries of something already in the gospel of Jesus Christ that we have not seen before or that we have forgotten. The new insights are not something added to the gospel but the further unpacking of the inexhaustible riches found in Jesus Christ. Of course, this is merely a place to begin theological argument. Much of the church's theology is an argument over whether one or another theological proposal is a new insight or a new (and therefore heretical) gospel.

[6]Some of the great works of theology have been produced in the context of cultural change: Augustine's *City of God* as the Roman Empire began to crumble; Thomas Aquinas's *Summa Theologiae* as Europe rediscovered Aristotle; Luther's and Calvin's works in a changing Europe. For an instructive and engaging account of a Christian encounter with another culture, see Vincent J. Donovan, *Christianity Rediscovered* (Maryknoll, N.Y.: Orbis, 1982). A contemporary example is the work of Lesslie Newbigin (*The Gospel in a Pluralist Society* [Grand Rapids, Mich.: Eerdmans, 1989]) in his "missionary encounter" with changing European culture.

[7]In *Philosophy and the Mirror of Nature* (Princeton, N.J.: Princeton University Press, 1979), Richard Rorty attacks the understanding and practice of philosophy that reflects and sustains traditional (that is, modernist) claims about human knowing.

[8]For Rorty the aim of philosophy should not be objective truth but ongoing conversation. He believes that the quest for objective knowledge treats humans as objects rather than as subjects and thereby suppresses or destroys our humanity. The quest for an ongoing conversation, by contrast, treats humans as subjects and thereby enables them to discover and fulfill their humanity (*Philosophy and the Mirror of Nature*, pp. 357-94).

[9]Richard Rorty, *Consequences of Pragmatism (Essays: 1972-1980)* (Minneapolis: University of Minnesota Press, 1982), esp. "World Well Lost," pp. 3-18.

[10]Ibid.

[11]See Richard Rorty, "The Priority of Democracy to Philosophy," in *Objectivism, Relativism and Truth: Philosophical Papers* (Cambridge: Cambridge University Press, 1991).

[12]The person who argues this most persistently and persuasively is Michel Foucault. Among his many works, see especially *The Order of Things: An Archaeology of the Human Sciences* (New York: Random House/Pantheon, 1971), *The Archaeology of Knowledge and the Discourse on Language*, trans. A. M. Sheridan Smith (New York: Pantheon, 1972), *Power/Knowledge: Selected Interviews and Other Writings 1972-1977*, trans. Colin

Gordon et al. (New York: Pantheon, 1980). Foucault is a complex thinker whose arguments I cannot treat adequately here. He does not reduce knowledge to power, but he does show how claims to knowledge are inextricably tied to the exercise of power.

[13]The *locus classicus* of the argument for the pervasiveness of interpretive, or "interpretative," communities is Stanley Fish, *Is There a Text in This Class? The Authority of Interpretive Communities* (Cambridge, Mass.: Harvard University Press, 1980).

[14]This is not to denigrate the issues engaged in these debates but to argue that the form of these debates is determined by our cultural situation: these debates are nothing more than struggles for power among competing interests groups.

[15]This result is not necessarily the intention of postmodernist thinkers, but it seems to be where the situation that they describe leads. Most postmodern thinkers do not recognize where we are headed because they lack a doctrine of sin. They have no saving response to where we are headed because they have no hope of redemption.

[16]In light of our recent history this postmodern hope seems as hopeless as the modern quest for certain knowledge. I will explore this hopelessness and propose a Christian response to it in chapters five and six.

[17]Although I am in sympathy with many of the concerns expressed by David Wells, I think that his books *No Place for Truth: Or, Whatever Happened to Evangelical Theology?* (Grand Rapids, Mich.: Eerdmans, 1993) and *God in the Wasteland: The Reality of Truth in a World of Fading Dreams* (Grand Rapids, Mich.: Eerdmans, 1995) represent this nostalgia.

[18]Many Christians are uncomfortable with the proposal that we abandon the language of "objective knowledge" or "objective truth." There are two reasons for this discomfort. First, as I have already warned, we have lived with modernity for a long time and have worked out a "comfortable living arrangement" with modernity. The breaking down of modernity exposes the errors that we have made in accommodating it. Therefore we must resist nostalgia for the past. Second, we fear that the only alternative to "objective truth" is subjectivity and relativism. I will seek to disarm this fear as we consider the temptation of postmodernity and as I develop my account of the virtue of faith.

[19]The story of how, in the age of modernity, Christian convictions have been marginalized or excluded by American universities is exhaustively and powerfully recounted in George Marsden, *The Soul of the American University: From Protestant Establishment to Established Unbelief* (New York: Oxford University Press, 1994).

[20]L. Gregory Jones, "A Thirst for God or Consumer Spirituality? Cultivating Disciplined Practices of Being Engaged by God," *Modern Theology* 13, no. 1 (January 1997): 3-28.

[21]For a trenchant analysis and critique of emotivism, see Alasdair MacIntyre, *After Virtue: A Study in Moral Theory,* 2nd ed. (Notre Dame, Ind.: University of Notre Dame Press, 1984), chap. 2.

[22]I recall vividly a casual remark of my teacher, Thomas Langford, that the problem with the contemporary debates over objectivism and relativism is that both make humans, rather than God, central. In my own theological terms, both are idolatrous. In many ways this chapter is merely my development of this remark, for which Dr. Langford should not be held responsible.

[23]For an early but still helpful philosophical analysis of this situation that also avoids the snare of epistemology, see Richard J. Bernstein, *Beyond Objectivism and Relativism: Science, Hermeneutics and Praxis* (Philadelphia: University of Pennsylvania Press, 1983). Most postmodernists would object to any characterization of them as relativists, for they claim to see relativism as a construct of the modernist quest for epistemological certainty.

[24]Although neither uses the language of virtue, two accounts powerfully argue positions similar to mine: Julian N. Hartt, "The Principle of Faith," in *A Christian Critique of American Culture: An Essay in Practical Theology* (New York: Harper & Row, 1967), pp. 145-64; and Lesslie Newbigin, *Truth to Tell: The Gospel as Public Truth* (Grand Rapids, Mich.: Eerdmans, 1991).

[25]In theology, "the person of Jesus Christ" is usually used to refer to our beliefs about his full divinity and full humanity. Here I am using the term in a broader sense to refer to his identity, his life, his death and his resurrection.

[26]Hans W. Frei, *The Identity of Jesus Christ: The Hermeneutical Bases of Dogmatic Theology* (Philadelphia: Fortress, 1975), is a tour de force in support of this assertion.

[27]Although he puts his argument in epistemological terms, Michael Polanyi gives a profound account of knowing as personal in his magisterial volume *Personal Knowledge: Toward a Post-Critical Philosophy* (New York: Harper & Row, 1958). Lesslie Newbigin makes extensive and accessible use of Polanyi's arguments in *Truth to Tell* and in *Foolishness to the Greeks: The Gospel and Western Culture* (Grand Rapids, Mich.: Eerdmans, 1986), chap. 4.

[28]Martin Buber, *I and Thou,* trans. Walter Kaufmann (New York: Scribner, 1970).

[29]Newbigin, *Truth to Tell,* p. 36.

[30]As noted earlier, in some parts of the Christian tradition, faith, hope and love are treated as theological virtues, meaning that they are virtues given by God that add something to human nature. Here I am suggesting that we do better if we think of these virtues as natural to the new life in Christ that is ours by God's gift.

[31]For a penetrating analysis of these differences, see Mark R. Schwehn, *Exiles from Eden: Religion and the Academic Vocation in America* (New York: Oxford University Press, 1993), pp. 5-16, 47-57.

[32]As Newbigin *(Truth to Tell)* notes, this kind of argument may cause considerable anger because "it threatens what have been accepted as axioms—namely the right and power of the human mind to make its own decisions about what is true" (p. 37).

[33]In the West our understanding of the church has been considerably corrupted by modernist understandings. To resist this corruption I will occasionally employ Douglas John Hall's term *disciple community* to designate what I mean by *church*. See Douglas John Hall, *Thinking the Faith: Christian Theology in a North American Context* (Minneapolis: Fortress, 1989), pp. 69-244, and *Confessing the Faith: Christian Theology in a North American Context* (Minneapolis: Fortress, 1996), pp. 33-340.

[34]For further arguments along the line taken here, see Jonathan R. Wilson, *Living Faithfully in a Fragmented World: Lessons for the Church from MacIntyre's "After Virtue"* (Valley Forge, Penn.: Trinity Press, forthcoming).

[35]This point may require some belaboring because we have such difficulty distinguishing between the mission of the church and "the American way of life." For further arguments in support of my assertion, see William Willimon and Stanley Hauerwas, *Resident Aliens: Life in the Christian Colony* (Nashville: Abingdon, 1989).

[36]See James M. Gustafson, *Treasure in Earthen Vessels: The Church as a Human Community* (Chicago: University of Chicago Press, 1961).

[37]For further description of the church, see Jonathan R. Wilson, *Theology as Cultural Critique: The Achievement of Julian Hartt* (Macon, Ga.: Mercer University Press, 1996), chap. 4.

[38]It is worth noting here that our conception of the church may need radical correction. During a children's sermon on Pentecost Sunday, the pastor of our congregation began talking about celebrating the birthday of the church. One of his listeners raised her hand and said, in effect, "Wait a minute, churches aren't born, they're built." I suspect that her comment reflects a prevalent popular misconception of the nature of the church.

[39]When we consider the case of a Christian (apparently) "isolated" from the church, two practices of the church take on greater significance: prayer for others, and visiting the sick and those who are in prison.

[40]This claim is further developed in chapters four, six and eight, where I describe practices of the church that form faith, sustain hope and teach love.

[41]For a practical description of this process, see John Howard Yoder, *The Priestly Kingdom: Social Ethics as Gospel* (Notre Dame, Ind.: University of Notre Dame Press, 1984), chap. 1, pp. 15-45.

[42]Even though modernity may claim that knowing is communal (scientists

verify through experimentation the conclusions of another scientist, philosophers correct the errors of another philosopher) the epistemology of modernity is still individualistic: I decide what is true for me.

[43]This assertion reflects my suspicion that the accusations of relativism and subjectivity make sense only if a person accepts the modernist construal of knowing. For a helpful analysis, see Phillip D. Kenneson, "There's No Such Thing as Objective Truth, and It's a Good Thing, Too," in *Christian Apologetics in the Postmodern World*, ed. Timothy R. Phillips and Dennis L. Okholm (Downers Grove, Ill.: InterVarsity Press, 1995), pp. 155-70.

[44]For further discussion of the gospel as a metanarrative in relation to postmodernity, see J. Richard Middleton and Brian J. Walsh, *Truth Is Stranger Than It Used to Be* (Downers Grove, Ill.: InterVarsity Press, 1995), chap. 5, and John Milbank, *Theology and Social Theory: Beyond Secular Reason* (Oxford: Basil Blackwell, 1990), chaps. 10-12.

[45]In another context Christians would go further: "It's not (just) who you know, it's (also) who knows you." J. I. Packer describes this in a classic passage from *Knowing God* (Downers Grove, Ill.: Inter-Varsity Press, 1973), p. 37: "What matters supremely, therefore, is not, in the last analysis, the fact that I know God, but the larger fact which underlies it—the fact that *He knows me*. I am graven on the palms of his hands. I am never out of his mind. All my knowledge of him depends upon his sustained initiative in knowing me. I know him, because he first knew me, and continues to know me. He knows me as a friend, one who loves me; and there is no moment when His eye is off me, or His attention distracted from me, and no moment, therefore, when His care falters." In the end, the One whom we know is the One who knows us. This truth collapses the questions of epistemology.

Chapter 4: Forming Faith

[1]The classic statement by Arthur F. Holmes (*The Idea of a Christian College*, rev. ed. [Grand Rapids, Mich.: Eerdmans, 1987]) contains many wise words. For example, "The question to ask about education is not 'What can I do with it?' That is the wrong question because it concentrates on instrumental values and reduces everything to a useful art. The right question is rather 'What can it do to me?'" (p. 29).

[2]In this chapter I use the phrases "faithful practice of education" and "faithful education" to represent the conviction that what I describe is a practice of education that both forms the virtue of faith and is formed by the virtue of faith.

[3]Thomas Howard, *Christ the Tiger: A Postscript to Dogma* (San Francisco: Ignatius, 1990).

[4]Three books have been particularly helpful: Craig R. Dykstra, *Vision and Character: A Christian Educator's Alternative to Kohlberg* (New York: Paulist, 1981); Henri J. M. Nouwen, *Creative Ministry* (Garden City, N.Y.:

Image, 1978); and Parker J. Palmer, *To Know As We Are Known: A Spirituality of Education* (San Francisco: Harper & Row, 1983).

[5] Alasdair MacIntyre, *After Virtue: A Study in Moral Theory,* 2nd ed. (Notre Dame, Ind.: University of Notre Dame Press, 1984), pp. 187-96.

[6] As we saw in chapter two, MacIntyre (*After Virtue,* p. 187) carefully delineates the connection between practices and virtues and sets them within the other elements of his account—a living tradition, a community and a conception of the *telos.* In *Transformed Judgment: Toward a Trinitarian Account of the Moral Life* (Notre Dame, Ind.: University of Notre Dame Press, 1990), pp. 76-79, L. Gregory Jones identifies two flaws in MacIntyre's account. First, MacIntyre does not see that friendship, especially friendship with God, is more determinative than practices for the formation of virtues. Second, MacIntyre treats the virtues as dependent on practices but does not see that the dependence also runs in the other direction—practices are also dependent on the virtues. These criticisms, however, do not lead Jones to abandon the concept of practices (see his use of the concept throughout his later book *Embodying Forgiveness*). In my account of the practice of education, I will seek to avoid these flaws in MacIntyre's account.

[7] This is one reason that I do not think our usual understanding of education is correct. It is just too simple to be a practice that forms virtue.

[8] When I consider worship as a practice in chapter six (under "Worship and the Church"), I will examine the relationship between practices and institutions.

[9] The book of Proverbs is an extended example of this truth. Consider the following: "Do not answer fools according to their folly, or you will be a fool yourself. Answer fools according to their folly, or they will be wise in their own eyes" (Prov 26:4-5). The only way to be faithful to both admonitions is through practical wisdom.

[10] One expression of "character development" is "outcome-based education." Like character development, this approach may be helpful. But it is also dangerous, because the "outcomes" that are sought do not represent the *telos* of the gospel.

[11] Two helpful theological critiques of "character development" are Dykstra, *Vision and Character,* and Stanley Hauerwas, *A Community of Character: Toward a Constructive Christian Social Ethic* (Notre Dame, Ind.: University of Notre Dame Press, 1981), chap. 7. For a description of character education in Christian colleges, see Arthur F. Holmes, *Shaping Character: Moral Education in the Christian College* (Grand Rapids, Mich.: Eerdmans, 1991). Although Holmes's account is helpful, it does not venture a description of the kind of character that we should be shaping.

[12] Hauerwas, *Community of Character,* p. 130.

[13] Mark R. Schwehn, *Exiles from Eden: Religion and the Academic Vocation*

in America (New York: Oxford University Press, 1993), p. 18. Although Schwehn focuses on the work of Max Weber, he takes Weber's work as representative of modernity. Schwehn's entire analysis follows lines similar to mine. In it he shows that the modernist approach to education results in alienation, loneliness and the absence of meaning—results precisely opposite those to which faith calls us.

[14]In Proverbs, wisdom is the virtue in view, but as we will see wisdom has the same characteristics as faith. Paul makes this connection in 1 Corinthians 1:18-31. I am indebted to Bruce Waltke, a wonderful teacher of the Old Testament and of wisdom, for directing my attention to the book of Proverbs, though he is not responsible for what I argue here.

[15]Derek Kidner, *Proverbs,* Tyndale Old Testament Commentaries, ed. D. J. Wiseman (London: Inter-Varsity Press, 1964), p. 36.

[16]For a brief and accessible treatment of these various Hebrew terms, see Kidner, *Proverbs,* pp. 36-37, and William P. Brown, *Character in Crisis: A Fresh Approach to the Wisdom Literature of the Old Testament* (Grand Rapids, Mich.: Eerdmans, 1998), pp. 23-30.

[17]Howard, *Christ the Tiger,* p. 65.

[18]See Brown, *Character in Crisis,* pp. 28-43.

[19]See the tour de force of John Milbank in *Theology and Social Theory: Beyond Secular Reason* (Oxford: Basil Blackwell, 1990).

[20]Although I will not pursue it here, the connection between wisdom and creation made in Proverbs 3:19-20 and 8:22-31 supports both my claim that the book of Proverbs exemplifies a practice of education that is cosmic and my denial of secularism.

[21]Commentators have noted numerous overlaps between the proverbs of Israel and the proverbs of other cultures, especially Egypt. This has led some commentators to describe at least some wisdom material as "secular," that is, as outside Israel's faith in Yahweh. But precisely the opposite dynamic is at work in the community of faith. Because of their belief that Yahweh is the God of the universe, all knowing is under his rule. See Brown, *Character in Crisis,* pp. 42-43.

[22]Brown, *Character in Crisis,* pp. 33-36. Brown unfortunately neglects the role of the mother in the teaching of wisdom (Prov 1:8; 6:20).

[23]Nouwen, *Creative Ministry,* pp. 3-20; Palmer, *To Know As We Are Known,* pp. 103-5.

[24]See Jones *(Transformed Judgment),* who explores, among other things, the role of friendship with God in the development of Christian character.

[25]Nouwen, *Creative Ministry,* pp. 8, 12-13, 17-18.

[26]Palmer, *To Know As We Are Known,* pp. 69-87.

[27]Although I will not pursue it here, the personification of Wisdom in Prov 8 and the wisdom Christology of some portions of the New Testament also support the connection that I am making between the book of

Proverbs and our practice of education as personal.

[28]For what follows, see Kidner, *Proverbs,* pp. 39-42. I am indebted to F. Leroy Forlines for first introducing me to the characters in the book of Proverbs.

[29]Nouwen, *Creative Ministry,* p. 19.

[30]Howard, *Christ the Tiger,* p. 142.

[31]I owe the term *blessed misfits* to James Houston. Sometime in the 1970s, Dr. Houston (then principal of Regent College) casually remarked to me in a conversation concerned primarily with other matters that his aim at Regent was to produce "well-adjusted misfits." That phrase has stayed with me and guided much of my ministry in the years since. The reason for my modification of the phrase will become clear as my account develops.

[32]*World* is, of course, an equivocal term in the New Testament. It is that which God loves (Jn 3:16), but it is also all that is in rebellion against him. Here I am using *world* in the latter sense.

[33]For further development of this claim, see Jonathan R. Wilson, *Living Faithfully in a Fragmented World: Lessons for the Church from MacIntyre's "After Virtue"* (Valley Forge, Penn.: Trinity Press, forthcoming).

[34]Some today call this temptation the "Constantinian temptation" or, more simply, "Constantinianism" (see Wilson, *Living Faithfully,* chap. 2; William Willimon and Stanley Hauerwas, *Resident Aliens: Life in the Christian Colony* [Nashville: Abingdon, 1989]; John Howard Yoder, "The Constantinian Sources of Western Social Ethics," in *The Priestly Kingdom: Social Ethics as Gospel* (Notre Dame, Ind.: University of Notre Dame Press, 1984), pp. 135-47, and "To Serve Our God and to Rule the World," in *Annual of the Society of Christian Ethics, 1988,* ed. D. M. Yeager (Washington, D.C.: Georgetown University Press, 1988), pp. 3-14.

[35]Stanley Hauerwas, *After Christendom: How the Church Is to Behave If Freedom, Justice and a Christian Nation Are Bad Ideas* (Nashville: Abingdon, 1991), chap. 4.

Chapter 5: Hope and the Christian Way of Being

[1]For evangelical differences, see Stanley J. Grenz, *The Millennial Maze* (Downers Grove, Ill.: InterVarsity Press, 1992), and Robert G. Clouse, ed. (with contributions by George Eldon Ladd, Herman A. Hoyt, Loraine Boettner and Anthony A. Hoekema), *The Meaning of the Millennium: Four Views* (Downers Grove, Ill.: InterVarsity Press, 1977). For a very different approach that still makes eschatology central, see the various works of Jürgen Moltmann, especially *Theology of Hope: On the Ground and Implications of Christian Eschatology,* trans. James W. Leith (New York and Evanston: Harper & Row, 1967) and *The Coming of God: Christian Eschatology,* trans. Margaret Kohl (Minneapolis: Fortress, 1996).

[2]For an exposure of this illusory hope, see three books by Jacques Ellul: *The Technological Society,* trans. John Wilkinson (New York: Knopf, 1964),

The Technological Bluff, trans. Geoffrey W. Bromiley (Grand Rapids, Mich.: Eerdmans, 1990), and *Hope in Time of Abandonment,* trans. C. Edward Hopkin (New York: Seabury, 1977).

[3]Though difficult, the best account of this postmodernist critique and the Christian response is found in John Milbank: *Theology and Social Theory: Beyond Secular Reason* (Oxford: Basil Blackwell, 1990), and *The Word Made Strange: Theology, Language, Culture* (Oxford: Basil Blackwell, 1997), chap. 2.

[4]In *The Postmodern Condition,* generally regarded as the foundational document of postmodernism, Jean-François Lyotard says, "Simplifying to the extreme, I define *postmodern* as incredulity toward metanarratives" (p. xiv). For an account of the gospel as a metanarrative that responds to postmodern incredulity, see J. Richard Middleton and Brian J. Walsh, *Truth Is Stranger Than It Used to Be* (Downers Grove, Ill.: InterVarsity Press, 1995).

[5]I am indebted to Stanley Hauerwas for this description of cynicism.

[6]For an account of postmodernity's ontology of violence, see Milbank, *Theology and Social Theory,* chap. 10. Whereas modernity recognizes the violence that marks the human condition and optimistically seeks to overcome it, postmodernity conceals the conviction that since the violence of the human condition is inescapable and ineradicable, we must learn to live with it.

[7]See the discussion of the "Constantinian temptation" in note 34 of chapter four.

[8]For an ontology of peace rooted in the gospel, see Milbank, *Theology and Social Theory,* chap. 12. Milbank roots his ontology of peace in creation. This needs to be completed by an ontology of peace rooted in redemption.

[9]Ellul, *Hope in Time of Abandonment,* p. 201.

[10]See further, Julian N. Hartt, *A Christian Critique of American Culture: An Essay in Practical Theology* (New York: Harper & Row, 1967), pp. 142-44.

[11]On the "coming of God," see Moltmann, *The Coming of God,* esp. pp. 22-28.

[12]In this situation the "craft of forgiveness" is also a necessary part of the Christian life. See L. Gregory Jones, *Embodying Forgiveness: A Theological Analysis* (Grand Rapids, Mich.: Eerdmans, 1995), esp. chap. 8.

[13]See Josef Pieper, *On Hope,* trans. Sister Mary Frances McCarthy (San Francisco: Ignatius, 1986), p. 21: "The virtue of hope is preeminently the virtue of the *status viatorus;* it is the proper virtue of the 'not yet.' " Also see Gabriel Marcel, *Homo Viator: Introduction to a Metaphysic of Hope,* trans. Emma Crauford (Gloucester, Mass: Peter Smith, 1978).

[14]See Stanley Hauerwas and Charles Pinches, *Christians Among the Virtues: Theological Conversations with Ancient and Modern Virtues* (Notre Dame, Ind.: University of Notre Dame Press, 1997), chap. 7.

[15]I return to the theme of righteousness when we consider hope as communal under the subhead "Hope as communal."

[16]See Moltmann, *Theology of Hope*, p. 31: "Hope makes us ready to bear 'the cross of the present.'"

[17]For profound remarks on how to read history, see John Howard Yoder, "To Serve Our God and to Rule the World," in *Annual of the Society of Christian Ethics, 1988,* ed. D. M. Yeager (Washington, D.C.: Georgetown University Press, 1988), esp. p. 11: "Hope is not a reflex rebounding from defeat but a reflection of theophany." By "theophany" Yoder refers here especially to the resurrection of Christ. "Defeat" is not meaningless, it is transformed by God in Christ.

[18]Although he does not have postmodernism directly in view, Moltmann (*Theology of Hope*) well describes the effect of its cynical "realism" when he says that "in adopting this so-called realism dictated by the facts we fall victim to the worst of all utopias—the utopia of the *status quo,* as R. Musil has called this kind of realism" (p. 23).

[19]When I consider the virtue of hope as communal, I will return to the righteousness of hope as a mark of the disciple community (see under "Hope as Communal").

[20]Paul is delightfully ambiguous in 2 Corinthians 5:17, which may be roughly translated "So if anyone is in Christ, new creation." Here I am drawing on the implication that those who are in Christ are new creations. Later, when we consider hope as cosmic, I will draw on the implication that if anyone is in Christ, the creation is made new. Both are supportable from this text and others.

[21]Since I will explore more fully the practice of the church that sustains hope in the next chapter, this section will be brief.

[22]See Moltmann, *Theology of Hope*, Part 5, "Exodus Church."

[23]This is not a "universalist" claim. The redemption of the world also involves the judgment and condemnation of some things to "the lake of fire" (Rev 20:13-15). Likewise, the reconciliation of all things to God means that all things will be put in their right relationship to God. For some things, this right relationship is exclusion from God's life.

[24]Commentators on this passage wrestle heroically with the application of "reconciliation" to "all things," since we properly think of reconciliation as directed to persons (see, for example, Peter T. O'Brien, *Colossians, Philemon,* Word Biblical Commentary 44 [Waco: Word, 1982], pp. 53-57). The comments of C. F. D. Moule (*The Epistles of Paul the Apostle to the Colossians and to Philemon: An Introduction and Commentary,* The Cambridge Greek Testament Commentary [Cambridge: At the University Press, 1968]) are apropos when he notes that although "the idea of reconciling to God 'everything'—the animate and the inanimate alike—is a difficult one for the modern reader. . . . Colossians includes the 'cosmic'

scene as well as the scene of man's salvation throughout this passage" (p. 71).

[25]Here I return to 2 Corinthians 5:17 and take up the other meaning of "new creation."

[26]Note that the command to subdue the earth and have dominion over it (Gen 1:28) is given to humanity before the Fall. It is one thing to tell sinless humanity to subdue and have dominion, it is quite another to say this to sinful, fallen humanity. Accounts of this command have not usually given enough attention to this difference.

[27]See James M. Houston, *I Believe in the Creator* (Grand Rapids, Mich.: Eerdmans, 1980), pp. 233-53.

[28]There is much more to be said on this topic. See Jonathan R. Wilson, "Evangelicals and the Environment: A Theological Concern," *Christian Scholar's Review* (forthcoming).

[29]I am indebted to Robert H. Gundry for whatever clarity and accuracy characterize this paragraph.

[30]After completing this chapter, I obtained a short study by C. F. D. Moule, *The Meaning of Hope: A Biblical Exposition with Concordance*, ed. John Reumann, Facet Books, Biblical Series 5 (Philadelphia: Fortress, 1963). Although Moule does not speak of hope as a virtue or attend directly to our cultural situation, his study supports my account of the virtue of hope.

Chapter 6: Sustaining Hope

[1]Eugene H. Peterson, *The Contemplative Pastor: Returning to the Art of Spiritual Direction* (Grand Rapids, Mich.: Eerdmans, 1993).

[2]Alasdair MacIntyre, *After Virtue: A Study in Moral Theory*, 2nd ed. (Notre Dame, Ind.: University of Notre Dame Press, 1984), pp. 193-96.

[3]Ibid., p. 194.

[4]Ibid.

[5]This is one reason that my account of a virtue precedes my account of the practice that forms and sustains virtue.

[6]Although he represents a tradition unfamiliar to many of us, the work of Alexander Schmemann (*For the Life of the World: Sacraments and Orthodoxy* [Crestwood, N.Y.: St. Vladimir's Seminary Press, 1973]) wonderfully captures the relation between worship and mission in the world.

[7]Stanley Hauerwas, *Vision and Virtue: Essays in Christian Ethical Reflection* (Notre Dame, Ind.: University of Notre Dame Press, 1981), chaps. 2, 12; Gilbert Meilaender, *The Theory and Practice of Virtue* (Notre Dame, Ind.: University of Notre Dame Press, 1984), chaps. 2-3.

[8]See my account of the "Therapist" in church life in Jonathan R. Wilson, *Living Faithfully in a Fragmented World: Lessons for the Church from MacIntyre's "After Virtue"* (Valley Forge, Penn.: Trinity Press, forthcoming), chap. 4. I draw on MacIntyre's description of the Therapist as one of the

"stock characters" of modernity. See MacIntyre, *After Virtue*, pp. 30-31.

[9]Philip Rieff, *The Triumph of the Therapeutic*, quoted in L. Gregory Jones, *Embodying Forgiveness: A Theological Analysis* (Grand Rapids, Mich.: Eerdmans, 1995), p. 43. The entire chapter in Jones's book is a trenchant critique of the "therapeutic corruption" of the Christian practice of forgiveness. See also, L. Gregory Jones, "A Thirst for God or Consumer Spirituality? Cultivating Disciplined Practices of Being Engaged by God," *Modern Theology* 13, no. 1 (January 1997).

[10]Here worship becomes an expression of our culture's thirst for *hyperreality*. Hyperreality is our quest to create a "reality" that is more "real" than reality. That is, hyperreality is our attempt to create a world that we dream of but never actually achieve. See Jean Baudrillard, *Simulacra and Simulation*, trans. Sheila Glaser (Ann Arbor: University of Michigan Press, 1994), and *America*, trans. Chris Turner (New York: W. W. Norton, 1989). Also see Umberto Eco, *Travels in Hyperreality: Essays*, trans. William Weaver (San Diego: Harcourt Brace, 1990). For an accessible account of hyperreality, see J. Richard Middleton and Brian J. Walsh, *Truth Is Stranger Than It Used to Be* (Downers Grove, Ill.: InterVarsity Press, 1995), pp. 37-42.

[11]John Howard Yoder, *The Politics of Jesus: Vicit Agnus Noster*, 2nd ed., rev. (Grand Rapids, Mich.: Eerdmans, 1994).

[12]For further development of this claim, see Robert E. Webber and Rodney Clapp, *People of the Truth: The Power of the Worshipping Community in the Modern World* (San Francisco: Harper & Row, 1988), esp. pt. 2, and Rodney Clapp, *A Peculiar People: The Church as Culture in a Post-Christian Society* (Downers Grove, Ill.: InterVarsity Press, 1996), esp. chap. 7, "The Church as Parade—The Politics of Liturgy."

[13]For a powerful development of the church's vocation in these terms, see Reinhard Hütter, "Midwife of History or Witness of the Eschaton?" *Journal of Religious Ethics* 18, no. 1 (Spring 1990): 27-54, and "Ecclesial Ethics, the Church's Vocation and Paraclesis," *Pro Ecclesia* 2, no. 4 (Fall 1993): 433-50.

[14]See Don E. Saliers, *Worship as Theology: Foretaste of Divine Glory* (Nashville: Abingdon, 1994), chap. 3 ("The Eschatological Character of Worship"), and Geoffrey Wainwright, *Eucharist and Eschatology* (New York: Oxford University Press, 1981).

[15]Saliers, *Worship as Theology*, pp. 173-90.

[16]In some traditions the liturgist calls on the people, "Lift up your hearts," and the people respond, "We lift them up." This call and response is not a call to overcome our anxieties by an act of the will. Rather, it is a call to place ourselves around the throne and to worship with the saints in heaven.

[17]Some may object that the previous description and this one are paradoxical, but they are no more or less paradoxical than the gospel claim that we are in Christ and that Christ is in us. These descriptions of worship, in fact, capture the tension of our present being as eschatological. In one

sense, we are already redeemed and participate in the life now in heaven. In another sense, we are not yet fully redeemed and so are still on this earth.

[18]Saliers, *Worship as Theology,* pp. 52-59.

[19]There are many controversies about sabbath keeping that we need not explore here. For a helpful account, see Dorothy C. Bass, "Keeping Sabbath," in *Practicing Our Faith: A Way of Life for a Searching People,* ed. Dorothy C. Bass (San Francisco: Jossey-Bass, 1997), pp. 75-89, bibliography, p. 209.

[20]Of course, some societies prohibit sabbath keeping. In these societies worship in the midst of another day of labor is a sign of hope for the eschaton that will free us from such tyranny. But in a society that supports sabbath keeping, not keeping the sabbath is a sign of hopelessness.

[21]See Saliers, *Worship as Theology,* pp. 75-76: "There is a 'deliberate rehearsal' at the heart of this process of bringing every aspect of character into harmony with God's intention for the world."

[22]Ibid., p. 117.

[23]Ibid., p. 111.

[24]F. Kefa Sempangi, with Barbara R. Thompson, *A Distant Grief* (Glendale, Calif.: Gospel Light Publications, 1979), p. 37.

[25]For more on this practice in East Africa, see F. Kefa Sempangi, "Walking in the Light," *Sojourners* 7, no. 2 (February 1978): 24-27. This practice has its dangers and is certainly not the only model for the practice of confession, but it does give us a concrete example on which to reflect.

[26]Jones, *Embodying Forgiveness,* pp. 71-98.

[27]Ibid., p. 299.

[28]Wendell Berry, *Collected Poems, 1957-1982* (San Francisco: North Point, 1984), p. 151.

[29]Ibid., p. 152.

[30]See Schmemann, *For the Life of the World.*

[31]Much more can be said about these acts than I will say here. My account is not meant to be exhaustive but rather suggests the connection between these acts and the formation of the virtue of hope. For further accounts, see Jones, *Embodying Forgiveness,* pp. 165-82, Saliers, *Worship as Theology,* pp. 56-61, Wainwright, *Eucharist and Eschatology.* We still lack a comprehensive treatment of footwashing. For a helpful study of the account in John 13, see John C. Thomas, *Footwashing in John 13 and the Johannine Community,* JSNT Supplement Series 61 (Sheffield, U.K.: JSOT, 1993).

[32]Saliers, *Worship as Theology,* p. 56.

[33]William H. Willimon, *The Service of God: How Worship and Ethics Are Related* (Nashville: Abingdon, 1983), pp. 95-117.

[34]By "live into our baptism" I mean that we become, by the transforming

work of the Holy Spirit, what we already are in Christ through our baptism. See Jones, *Embodying Forgiveness,* pp. 166-75.

[35]See the further discussion of Communion in chapter eight under "Hospitality as Communal."

[36]See the discussion in chapter five, pp. 109-10.

Chapter 7: Love and the Christian Way of Doing

[1]One of the most popular and accessible treatments is C. S. Lewis, *The Four Loves* (New York: Harcourt Brace Jovanovich, 1960).

[2]For example, Lewis (ibid., pp. 11-21) contrasts "need-love" and "gift-love." Others wrestle with the apparently contrasting claims of friendship *(philia)* and "love" *(agapē);* for a helpful treatment of this discussion, see Paul J. Waddell, *Friendship and the Moral Life* (Notre Dame, Ind.: University of Notre Dame Press, 1989), pp. 70-119.

[3]This is the argument of "situation ethics" as presented by Joseph Fletcher, *Situation Ethics* (Philadelphia: Westminster Press, 1966).

[4]In *The Four Loves* Lewis clearly distinguishes affection (Greek *storgē),* friendship *(philia),* eros *(eros)* and charity *(agapē).*

[5]A classic example of this is the strong contrast, indeed, the rivalry, drawn between *agapē* and *eros* in Anders Nygren, *Agapē and Eros: The Christian Idea of Love,* trans. Philip S. Watson (1930-1936; reprint, Chicago: University of Chicago Press, 1953). For a critique of this and other classic accounts of love, see Gene Outka, *Agapē: An Ethical Analysis* (New Haven, Conn.: Yale University Press, 1972).

[6]Here I am seeking to resolve a difficult issue very briefly. For a contemporary discussion of these difficulties, see Edmund N. Santurri and William Werpehowski, eds., *The Love Commandments: Essays in Christian Ethics and Moral Philosophy* (Washington, D.C.: Georgetown University Press, 1992), and Colin Grant, "For the Love of God: Agape," *Journal of Religious Ethics* 24, no. 1 (Spring 1996): 3-21, and responses, pp. 22-46. My main point is simply that thinking of love as a virtue would dissolve much of the difficulties by teaching us that all forms of love act in all relations in ways appropriate to their *telos,* the eschaton of God. When our thinking is teleological, the difficulties may be resolved.

[7]For an account of how the gospel transforms our affection for family that can easily become idolatry, see Rodney Clapp, *Families at the Crossroads* (Downers Grove, Ill.: InterVarsity Press, 1993). For an account of how the gospel transforms our friendships, see L. Gregory Jones, *Transformed Judgment: Toward a Trinitarian Account of the Moral Life* (Notre Dame, Ind.: University of Notre Dame Press, 1990), pp. 73-119, and Waddell, *Friendship and the Moral Life.*

[8]This language may give the appearance that I am endorsing situation ethics. I am not. For a critique of situation ethics, see below, pp. 146-47.

[9]All quotes in this paragraph are from St. Thomas Aquinas, *Treatise on the Virtues*, trans. John A. Oesterle (Notre Dame, Ind.: University of Notre Dame Press, 1984), p. 123. The passage is from the *Summa Theologiae* I-II, question 62, article 4. The explanation of love as the form of the virtues is found later in the *Summa Theologiae* II-II, question 23, articles 7 and 8.

[10]For a helpful discussion, see Robert C. Roberts, *Spirituality and Human Emotion* (Grand Rapids, Mich.: Eerdmans, 1982).

[11]For a helpful account of the character of God as the one who commands, see Richard J. Mouw, *The God Who Commands* (Notre Dame, Ind.: University of Notre Dame Press, 1990), chap. 8, "The Triune Commander."

[12]This is, roughly speaking, the claim of situation ethics.

[13]See chapter two, pp. 39-41.

[14]I am indebted to my late teacher, Klaus Bockmühl, for this insight.

[15]Here the task of theological ethics becomes that of supporting the mission of the church to bear witness to the gospel of Jesus Christ. The purpose of Christian ethics is not to make us better people but to make us more faithful witnesses.

[16]See the marvelous meditations by Peter Kreeft, *Love Is Stronger Than Death* (San Francisco: Ignatius, 1992).

[17]See the "ontology of peace" in John Milbank, *Theology and Social Theory: Beyond Secular Reason* (Oxford: Basil Blackwell, 1990), pp. 422-34. Milbank's counter-ontology of the peaceableness of creation needs to be complemented by a "counter-ontology of the peaceableness of redemption." I plan to give that account in a future article tentatively entitled "Toward a More Catholic and *Evangelical* Faith: Reflections on Milbank's *Theology and Social Theory*."

[18]Miroslav Volf, *Exclusion and Embrace: A Theological Exploration of Identity, Otherness and Reconciliation* (Nashville: Abingdon, 1996). Volf's work is a wonderful testimony to the gospel of peace and reconciliation in the midst of an unjust, violent world.

[19]Here I am drawing on H. Richard Niebuhr, *The Responsible Self: An Essay in Christian Moral Philosophy*, with an introduction by James M. Gustafson (San Francisco: Harper & Row, 1963): "Responsibility affirms: 'God is acting in all actions upon you. So respond to all actions upon you as to respond to his action' " (p. 126). The problem with Niebuhr's account is that it is grounded in a phenomenological analysis of the human condition, not in the gospel.

[20]Perkins tells his story in a number of places. The fullest account is John Perkins, *Let Justice Roll Down* (Glendale, Calif.: Gospel Light, 1976).

[21]Ibid., p. 218.

[22]See, for example, one version of Kant's "categorical imperative": "Act so that you treat humanity, whether in your own person or in that of another,

always as an end and never as a means only." Immanuel Kant, *Foundations of the Metaphysics of Morals,* trans. with an introduction by Lewis White Beck (New York: Macmillan, 1985), p. 47.

[23]See John Howard Yoder, "Peace Without Eschatology?" in *The Royal Priesthood: Essays Ecclesiological and Ecumenical,* ed. Michael G. Cartwright (Grand Rapids, Mich.: Eerdmans, 1994), pp. 144-67.

[24]Robert H. Gundry, *"Sōma" in Biblical Theology: With Emphasis on Pauline Anthropology* (Cambridge: Cambridge University Press, 1976; reprint, Grand Rapids, Mich.: Zondervan, 1987), p. 39.

[25]For a profound exploration of our inability to grasp the "causal joint" between God and humanity, see Austin Farrer, *Faith and Speculation: An Essay in Philosophical Theology* (London: A. & C. Black, 1967; reprint, Edinburgh: T & T Clark, 1988).

[26]Perkins, *Let Justice Roll Down,* p. 57.

[27]Roberta C. Bondi, *To Love As God Loves: Conversations with the Early Church* (Philadelphia: Fortress, 1987), p. 20.

[28]This assertion does not mean that we are free to treat those outside the gospel as "less than human." Rather, it puts an end to all evaluations of human worth that are not shaped by the gospel. This enables us to acknowledge differences among us without in any way diminishing anyone's worth. The good news is that all of us are loved by God. That gospel is the basis of our worth and the criterion of our love.

[29]John Perkins, *With Justice for All* (Ventura, Calif.: Regal, 1982).

[30]Although I would want to give a more theological account, the work of Charles Taylor is a powerful reading of this characteristic of modernity. See especially Charles Taylor, *Sources of the Self: The Making of Modern Identity* (Cambridge, Mass: Harvard University Press, 1989).

Chapter 8: Teaching Love

[1]When friends come home from short-term mission trips, they often marvel at the hospitality they have received from people who have less than they. This kind of experience exposes the limitations of our prosperity. If my friends weren't prosperous, they might not have made the trip. Then again, if they weren't prosperous they might be freer to engage in mission without having to take a trip.

[2]Rowan A. Greer, *Broken Lights and Mended Lives: Theology and Common Life in the Early Church* (University Park: Pennsylvania State University Press, 1986), p. 130.

[3]See Letty M. Russell, *Church in the Round: Feminist Interpretation of the Church* (Louisville, Ky.: Westminster John Knox Press, 1993): "Christian communities fear difference sufficiently that they usually spend a considerable amount of time tending the margins or boundaries of their communities, not in order to *connect* with those outside but, rather, to

protect themselves from strangers. Sometimes discussions of church membership are more concerned with who is in or out than with how to be an open and welcoming community" (p. 176).

[4]Christine Pohl, "Hospitality from the Edge: The Significance of Marginality in the Practice of Welcome," *The Annual of the Society of Christian Ethics* 1995, p. 135.

[5]In the next section we will consider social structure in relation to the postmodernist notion of "difference."

[6]For an account of this, see Parker J. Palmer, *The Company of Strangers: Christians and the Renewal of America's Public Life* (New York: Crossroad, 1992), Michael Ignatieff, *The Needs of Strangers* (New York: Viking, 1985), and Robert N. Bellah et al., *Habits of the Heart: Individualism and Commitment in American Life* (New York: Harper & Row, 1986).

[7]Henri J. M. Nouwen, *Reaching Out: The Three Movements of the Spiritual Life* (Garden City, N.Y.: Doubleday, 1975), p. 46.

[8]Francis Schaeffer long ago issued a prophetic call to the practice of hospitality that entails risk in *The Church at the End of the 20th Century* (Downers Grove, Ill.: InterVarsity Press, 1970), pp. 103-12. Schaeffer's call has integrity through the ministry of L'Abri.

[9]Postmodernity is sometimes misinterpreted as an emphasis on hyperindividualism. But hyperindividualism is an expression of hypermodernity, not an expression of postmodernity, which effaces the individual.

[10]I am not presuming that the practice of hospitality provides easy, straightforward resolutions of these issues. I am arguing that fear and hostility, which have no place in the virtue of love and the practice of hospitality, typically determine the way in which we frame and carry on these debates.

[11]This is not to deny the hospitality offered by many nurses and some doctors. But in most instances those who offer hospitality do so in spite of the institution and in some cases in the face of hostility to the practice of hospitality.

[12]One place to look for an example is the various AIDS ministries that have developed in recent years. See Letty Russell, *The Church with AIDS: Renewal in the Midst of Crisis* (Louisville, Ky.: Westminster John Knox Press, 1990).

[13]See John Koenig, *New Testament Hospitality: Partnership with Strangers as Promise and Mission* (Philadelphia: Fortress, 1985).

[14]Also later, when I consider hospitality as a work of the Spirit in us, we will see how this passage reminds us that God's hospitality is not our own achievement.

[15]Rowan Williams, *Resurrection: Interpreting the Easter Gospel* (New York: Pilgrim, 1984), pp. 76-99, and Koenig, *New Testament Hospitality*, p. 5.

[16]For many of us this will call to mind the hospitality practiced by Mother

Teresa and the Sisters of Charity, who see in those for whom they care the face of Jesus Christ.

[17]Williams, *Resurrection,* pp. 106-15.

[18]Stanley Hauerwas, *The Peaceable Kingdom: A Primer in Christian Ethics* (Notre Dame, Ind.: University of Notre Dame Press, 1983), p. 143.

[19]Pohl, "Hospitality from the Edge," pp. 121-22.

[20]See Philip Hallie, *Lest Innocent Blood Be Shed: The Story of the Village of Le Chambon and How Goodness Happened There* (San Francisco: Harper & Row, 1980), and the film *Weapons of the Spirit,* directed by Pierre Sauvage (New York: First Run/Icarus Films, 1987).

[21]Philip Haillie, "From Cruelty to Goodness," *The Hastings Center Report* 11 (1981): 26-27, quoted in Koenig, *New Testament Hospitality,* p. 143.

[22]Nouwen, *Reaching Out,* p. 51.

[23]In addition to the French village of Le Chambon, which I will consider below, among the many communities that practice hospitality, three that stand out are L'Abri, L'Arche and the Catholic Worker Movement founded by Dorothy Day. For L'Abri, see the books by Francis A. Schaeffer, the history by Edith Schaeffer (*L'Abri,* expanded ed. [Wheaton, Ill.: Crossway, 1992]) and a perceptive essay by Michael Hamilton, "The Dissatisfaction of Francis Schaeffer," *Christianity Today* 41, no. 3 (March 3, 1997): 22-30. For L'Arche, see Jean Vanier, *An Ark for the Poor: The Story of L'Arche* (New York: Crossroad, 1995), and his other writings. For the Catholic Worker Movement, see the writings of Dorothy Day and the works of William D. Miller, *A Harsh and Dreadful Love: Dorothy Day and the Catholic Worker Movement* (Garden City, N.Y.: Image/Doubleday, 1974), and *Dorothy Day: A Biography* (San Francisco: Harper & Row, 1982).

[24]Stephen E. Fowl and L. Gregory Jones, *Reading in Communion: Scripture and Ethics in the Christian Life* (Grand Rapids, Mich.: Eerdmans, 1991), p. 73.

[25]Koenig, *New Testament Hospitality,* p. 143.

Index of Names and Subjects

Index of Scripture